ERNST TOLLER

VORMORGEN

THE COLLECTED POEMS

TRANSLATED BY
MATHILDA CULLEN

the operating system's unlimited editions
GLOSSARIUM : UNSILENCED TEXTS x kin(d)*
print//document

VORMORGEN :
THE COLLECTED POEMS OF ERNST TOLLER

ISBN: 978-1-946031-69-3
Library of Congress CIP Number: 2021940235

edited and designed by Mathilda Cullen & Elæ Moss
using the Operating System Open Design Protocol

As of 2020 all titles are available for donation-only download via our Open Access Library: www.theoperatingsystem.org/os-open-access-community-publications-library/

The Operating System is a member of the **Radical Open Access Collective**, a community of scholar-led, not-for-profit presses, journals and other open access projects. Now consisting of 40 members, we promote a progressive vision for open publishing in the humanities and social sciences.

Learn more at: http://radicaloa.disruptivemedia.org.uk/about/

This text was set in Grotesk, Alegreya, OCR-A Standard, and Futíða. Grotesk is used via a SIL Open Font License, through Velvetyne Type Foundry. It was designed by Frank Adebiaye, Velvetyne's founder. All type on VTF is libre and open-source, and fully aligned with the OS's mission. Support their work and learn more at https://velvetyne.fr

Cover design by Angelo Maneage with Elæ Moss
https://angelomaneagethewebsite.com/
maneageatrois@gmail.com

Your donation makes our publications, platform and programs possible! We <3 You.
http://theoperatingsystem.org/subscribe-join/

the operating system
www.theoperatingsystem.org
operator@theoperatingsystem.org
IG: @the_operating_system
tweettweet: @the_os_

ERNST TOLLER

VORMORGEN

THE COLLECTED POEMS

TRANSLATED BY
MATHILDA CULLEN

GLOSSARIUM : UNSILENCED TEXTS
unlimited editions @ THE OS c. 2021

for Margo, Abbey, and Dom
who've heard me talk Toller more than anyone else,
and who nourished me through this project from its infancy.

all my thanks to Irene Zanol of the Ernst Toller society,
for helping me find these poems and all her transatlantic love.

to Lee Schlesinger, for his love of etymology
and for enjoying my mistranslations.

all power, all solidarity to the poets
unsung of history they who sing it.

INHALT / CONTENTS

IN MEMORY OF ERNST TOLLER

W. H. AUDEN

The shining neutral summer has no voice
To judge America, or ask how a man dies;
And the friends who are sad and the enemies who rejoice

Are chased by their shadows lightly away from the grave
Of one who was egotistical and brave,
Lest they should learn without suffering how to forgive.

What was it, Ernst, that your shadow unwittingly said?
O did the child see something horrid in the woodshed
Long ago? Or had the Europe which took refuge in your head

Already been too injured to get well?
O for how long,like the swallows in that other cell,
Had the bright little longings been flying in to tell

About the big friendly death outside,
Where people do not occupy or hide;
No towns like Munich; no need to write?

Dear Ernst, lie shadowless at last among
The other war-horses who existed till they'd done
Something that was an example to the young.

We are lived by powers we pretend to understand:
They arrange our loves; it is they who direct at the end
The enemy bullet, the sickness, or even our hand.

It is their tomorrow hangs over the earth of the living
And all that we wish for our friends; but existing is believing
We know for whom we mourn and who is grieving.

GEDICHTE DER GEFANGENEN

POEMS OF THE IMPRISONED

Kamerad,
in jeder Stadt, in
jedem Dorf begleitet dich
ein Gefängnis

Den namenlosen Toten
deutscher Revolution

Wer die Pfade bereitet,
stirbt an der Schwelle.
Doch es neigt sich vor ihm
in Ehrfurcht der Tod.

Comrade,
in every city, in
every village a prison
goes with you

To the nameless dead
of the German revolution.

Who pioneers the path,
dies on the threshold.
Though it it slants before him
in reverence of death.

An Die Freunde.
Was ist ein Jahr und was ist eine Stunde,
Im Acker Zeit, der brach zu unsern Füßen liegt.

„Es kann nichts entsetzlicher sein,
als daß die Handlungen eines Menschen
unter dem Willen eines andern stehen sollen."
— Kant, Fragmente VIII

„Trotzdem sie nur von Gesetzen reden: auch das
Gesetz ist nicht frei von Menschlichkeit. Das Gesetz ist
für uns Menschen nicht dazu gemacht, andern Menschen durch Ekel oder
Schmerz das Leben zu nehmen."
— Kleist

Dearest friends,
What is a year and what is an hour,
in the time of the field that lies fallow under our feet.

"It cannot be more appalling than for
the actions of one man
to stand under the will of another."
— Kant, fragment VIII

"Nonetheless, they speak only of laws:
even the law is not free from humanity.
The law is not made for us humans to take the lives of
other people through disgust or pain."
— Kleist

SCHLAFLOSE NACHT

Metallne Schritte in die Nächte fallen,
Die Posten buckeln durch die Höfe ohne Rast.
Oh, jeder Schlag ist Herzschlag ungeheurer Last,
Die uns bedrängt mit immer scharfen Krallen.

Wir lauschen schlaflos in das starre Hallen,
Ein schwarzes Schweigen wächst im schwarzen Glast,
Deß toter Atem fröstelnd uns umfaßt,
Zermartert Blicke an die Eisengitter prallen.

Warum, mein Bruder, feindlich durch die Höfe schreiten?
Uns alle band ein Schicksal an den gleichen Pfahl,
Uns alle eint der Kreaturen tausendjährge Qual,

Uns alle wirbelt dunkler Zwang durch die Gezeiten.
Oh, Fluch gesetzter Grenzen! Menschen hassen ohne Wahl!
Du, Bruder Tod, wirst uns vereint geleiten.

DURCHSUCHUNG UND FESSELUNG

(Dem Andenken des erschoßnen
Kameraden Dorfmeister, München)

Den nackten Leib brutalen Blicken preisgegeben,
Betastet uns ein schamlos Greifen feiler Hände,
In Fratzenbündel splittern graue Wände,
Die wie Gepfeil gen unsre Herzen streben.

Pflockt Arm und Fuß in rostige Kette,
Brennt Narben ein den magren Händen,
Ihr könnt, Ihr könnt den Leib nicht schänden,
Wir stehen frei an der verfehmten Stätte!

So standen vor uns all die Namenlosen,
Rebellen wider des Jahrhunderts Tyrannei,
Auf Sklavenschiffen meuternde Matrosen —

Der Promethiden ewig trotziger Schrei!
So standen sie an Mauern der Geweihten.
So starben sie am Rande der verheißnen Zeiten.

SLEEPLESS NIGHT

Metallic footsteps falling in the night,
The guards arched over through the yards without rest.
Oh, each beat, heartbeating colossal weight
That presses in on us with claws, sharpening.

We eavesdrop sleepless in rigid halls,
A black silence rises from black glass,
A shivering dead breath embraces us,
Agonized glances collide with iron grating.

Why, my brother, striding hostile through the fields?
We're all tied to the same stake of fate,
We're all united by the creature's thousand year torment,

We're all spun darkly through the tides.
Oh, fuck set borders! People hate without choice!
You, brother Death, will lead us into unity.

SEARCH AND CAPTURE

(to the memory of an executed
comrade, Dorfmeister, Munich)

Brutal glances exposed the naked body,
A shameless gripping of feeble hands touches us,
Gray walls shiver in a grotesque bundle
Which, like the arrows of our hearts, take aim.

Arms and feet fastened in rusted chains,
Burn scars on skinny hands,
They can, they cannot desecrate the body,
We stand free on the defiled site!

So stood before us, all the Nameless
Rebels against the century's tyranny
From slave ships, those mutinous sailors —

The supplies' eternal defiant cry!
So they stood on the walls of devotion.
So they died on the verge of the promised times.

WÄLDER

Ihr Wälder fern an Horizonten schwingend,
Vom abendlichen Hauche eingehüllt,
Wie meine Sehnsucht friedlich euch erfüllt,
Minuten Schmerz der Haft bezwingend.

Ich presse meine Stirne an die Eisensäulen,
Die Hände rütteln ihre Unrast wund,
Ich bin viel ärmer als ein armer Hund,
Ich bin des angeschoßnen Tieres hilflos Heulen.

Ihr Buchenwälder, Dome der Bedrückten,
Ihr Kiefern, Melodie der Heimat, tröstet Leid,
Wie wobet ihr geheimnisvoll um den beglückten

Knaben der fernen Landschaft wundersames Kleid ...
Wann werde ich, umarmt vom tiefen Rauschen,
Den hohen Psalmen eurer Seele lauschen?

SPAZIERGANG DER STRÄFLINGE

(Dem Andenken des erschoßnen
Kameraden Wohlmuth, München)

Sie schleppen ihre Zellen mit in stumpfen Blicken
Und stolpern, lichtentwöhnte Pilger, im Quadrat,
Proleten, die im Steinverließ ersticken,
Proleten, die ein Paragraph zertrat.

Im Eck die Wärter träg und tückisch lauern.
Von Sträuchern, halb verkümmert, rinnt ein trübes Licht
Und kriecht empor am Panzer starrer Mauern,
Betastet schlaffe Körper und zerbricht.

Vorm Tore starb der Stadt Gewimmel.
„Am Unrathaufen wird im Frühling Grünes sprießen ...“
Denkt Einer, endet mühsam die gewohnte Runde,

Verweilt und blinzelt matt zum Himmel:
Er öffnet sich wie bläulich rote Wunde,
Die brennt und brennt und will sich nimmer schließen.

WOODS

Their forests swinging far on the horizon
Shrouded in the evening's breath
As my desire quietly meets you,
Minutes to conquer the pain of imprisonment.

I press my forehead against the iron pillars,
Hands shaking their restlessness raw.
I am much poorer than a poor dog.
I am the shot animal's helpless howls.

Your Buchenwalds, domes of the oppressed.
Your pines, melody of the homeland, comforting pain,
How you weaved a wondrous dress secretly

Around the blessed boy in the distant landscape —
When will I, enveloped in the deep static,
Listen to the high psalms of your soul?

WALK OF THE CONVICTS

(to the memory of Comrade
Wohlmuth, executed in Munich)

They lug their cells with dulled looks
And stumble, light-worshipping pilgrims, in the square.
Proles who were smothered in the stone dungeon,
Proles who trampled a paragraph.

In the corner the watchmen lurk, lazy and treacherous.
From the bushes, half-withered, leaks a dull light
And creeps up the shells of numb walls,
Touches shattered bodies, and breaks.

The crowd died before the gates of the city.
One thinks, "In the spring, Green will sprout
From the trash," the usual patrol ends arduously,

Lingers, and blinks feebly at the sky:
He opens like a bluish-red wound,
That burns and burns and never wants to shut.

BEGEGNUNG IN DER ZELLE

Die Dinge, die erst feindlich zu dir schauen,
Als wären sie in Späherdienst gezwängte Schergen,
Sie laden dich zu Fahrten ein gleich guten Fergen,
Und hegen dich wie schwesterliche Frauen.

Es nähern sich dir all die kargen Dinge:
Die schmale Pritsche kommt, die blauen Wasserkrüge,
Der Schemel flüstert, daß er gern dich trüge,
Die Wintermücken wiegen sich wie kleine Schmetterlinge.

Und auch das Gitterfenster kommt, das du verloren,
Mit Augen, die sich an den schwarzen Stäben stachen,
Anstarrtest, während deine Arme hilflos brachen,

Und Köpfe der Erschoßnen wuchsen aus versperrten Toren.
Das Gitterfenster ruft: Nun, Lieber, schaue, schaue,
Wie ich aus Wolken dir ein Paradies erbaue.

LIED DER EINSAMKEIT

Sie wölbt um meine Seele Kathedralen,
Sie schäumt um mich wie brandend Meer,
Der Gosse sperrt sie sich wie eine Wehr,
Und wie ein Wald beschützt sie meine Qualen.

In ihr fühl' ich die Süße abendlicher Stille,
Auf leeren Stunden blüht sie maienliches Feld,
Ihr Schoß gebiert das Wunder der geahnten Welt,
Ein stählern Schwert steilt sich metallner Wille.

Sie schmiegt sich meinem Leib wie schlanker Frauen Hände,
In meine Sehnsucht perlt sie aller Märchen Pracht,
Ein sanftes Schwingen wird sie hingeträumter Nacht...

Doch ihre Morgen lodern Brände,
Sie sprengen Tore schwerer Alltagszelle,
Einstürzen Räume, aufwächst eisige Helle.

ENCOUNTER IN THE CELL

All the things that first seemed hostile to you
As if they were spies, henchmen. They
Invite you on rides like good ferrymen
And cherish you like sisterly women.

All the empty things approaching you:
The cramped beds come, blue jugs of water,
The stool whispers that he likes to carry you,
The winter mosquitos weigh the same as butterflies.

And the grated windows come too, which you lost
With eyes stabbing through black bars,
Staring, while your arms helplessly broke

And the heads of those shot dead rise on locked gates.
The barred window cries: Now love, behold, behold
How I will build you a paradise from clouds

SONG OF SOLITUDE

It curves cathedrals round my soul,
It froths around me like the surging sea.
The gutter locks it in like a dam
And, like a forest, contains my agonies.

In her I can feel the sweetness of the evening silence,
On the empty hours she blooms the may field.
Her womb births a wonder to the fearing world;
A steel sword plunges its metallic will.

It clings to my body like a slender women's hands.
In my yearning she pearls all the glory of fairy tales.
A gentle sway and she becomes dreamlike night —

But her mornings, blazing fires
Breaking open the heavy cell gates;
An icy brightness emerges from collapsing rooms

GEFANGENE MÄDCHEN

Wie kleine arme Dirnen an belebten Straßenecken
Sich schüchtern fast und wieder roh bewegen,
Im Schatten der Laternen sich erst dreister regen
Und den zerfransten Rock kokett verstecken ...

Wie Waisenkinder, die geführt auf Promenaden,
Je zwei und zwei in allzu kurzen grauen
Verschoßnen Kleidern sehr verschämt zu Boden schauen
Und Stiche fühlen in den nackten Waden ...

So schlürfen sie umstellt von hagren Wärterinnen,
Die warmen Hüften wiegend auf asphaltnen Kreisen,
Sie streichen heimlich mit Gebärden, leisen,

Das härne Kleid, als strichen sie plissiertes Linnen,
Und wie sich in gewölbten Händen Brüste runden,
Befällt sie Grauen ob der Last der leeren Stunden ...

FABRIKSCHORNSTEINE AM VORMORGEN

(Dem Andenken des erschoßnen
Kameraden Lohmar, München)

Sie stemmen ihre schwarze Wucht in Dämmerhelle,
Gepanzert recken sie sich drohendsteil,
Sie spalten zarte Nebel wie getriebner Keil,
Daß jeder warme Hauch um sie zerschelle.

Aus ihren Mäulern kriechen schwarze Schlangen
In blasse Fernen, die ein Silberschleier hüllt.
Sie künden lautlos: „Wir sind Burg und Schild!
Die Gluten winden sich, in uns gefangen."

Der Morgen kündet sich mit violettem Lachen,
Den Himmel füllt ein tiefes Blau,
Da gleichen sie verfrornen Posten, überwachen,

Und werden spitz und kahl und grau,
Und stehen hilflos da und wie verloren
Im lichten Äther, den ein Gott geboren.

GIRLS IMPRISONED

Like poor little whores on busy street corners
Almost shy and again move raw.
Impudent rain in the shadows of the lamplight,
and those frayed skirts coyly hidden —

Like orphans on parade,
Two and two in all too short gray
Faded dresses, looking to the floor in shame
And the stings on their bare calves —

So they drink, surrounded by the guards,
Warm hips swinging against asphalt posts,
They stroke quietly with soft gestures

Stroking the hair dress as if it were pleated linen
And with her round breasts in curved hands
She dreads the weight of the empty hours —

SMOKESTACKS AT DAWN

(in memory of comrade Lohmar,
executed in Munich)

They lift their black weight at daybreak,
Armored, ominous, they reach,
Splitting the soft fog like a wedge driven in
As every warm breath shatters around them.

Black snakes crawl from their mouths
In the pale distance, wrapped in a silver veil.
Soundless, they announce: "We are castle and shield!
The fires squirm, trapped inside us!"

With violet laughter the morning is announced.
A deep blue fills the sky,
There they resemble the frozen guards, watching,

And become sharp and bleak and gray,
And stand there, helpless and lost
In the light ether that birthed a god.

DIE MAUER DER ERSCHOSSENEN
PIETÁ, STADELHEIM, 1919

Wie aus dem Leib des heiligen Sebastian,
Dem tausend Pfeile tausend Wunden schlugen,
So Wunden brachen aus Gestein und Fugen,
Seit in den Sand ihr Blut verlöschend rann.

Vor Schrei und Aufschrei krümmte sich die Wand,
Vor Weibern, die mit angeschoßnen Knien „Herzschuß!“ flehten,
Vor Männern, die getroffen sich wie Kreisel drehten,
Vor Knaben, die um Gnade weinten mit zerbrochner Hand.

Da solches Morden raste durch die Tage,
Da Erde wurde zu bespienem Schoß,
Da trunkenes Gelächter kollerte von Bajonetten,

Da Gott sich blendete und arm ward, nackt und bloß,
Sah man die schmerzensreiche Wand in großer Klage
Die toten Menschenleiber an ihr steinern Herze betten.

DER GEFANGENE UND DER TOD

(Meinem lieben Zellennachbarn Valtin Hartig)

Der Gefangene spricht:

Ich denke deinen Namen, Tod, und um mich bricht
Der Zellenbau in Trümmer, Fundamente liegen bloß,
Aus Pfosten reißen sich die schweren Eisengitter los
Und krümmen sich im maskenlosen starren Licht.

In meiner Seele gellt ein Schrei. Ein Zittern wirft
verschüchterte Gebärde
Ins Blut, darin das Leben pochend schwingt —
Und wie die Kreißende um sich und um ihr Junges ringt,
So ringt mein Blut verzweifelt um den Quell der Erde.

Oh, daß ich fliehen könnte! Denn dir hilflos hingegeben,
Heißt hilflos sich zerstören. Wer sich aufgibt,
Wählt dich zum Freund. Ich aber will das Leben!

THE WALL OF THE EXECUTED
PIETÁ, STADELHEIM, 1919

Like out of the corpse of St. Sebastian
Thousands of arrows met thousands of wounds
Wounds broke out of brick and mortar
Since her blood ran in the sand, fading.

Before the screams and clamor the wall convulsed,
Before women shot in the knees plead "Execution!"
Before men spinning like tops fell over,
Before children crying for mercy with broken hands.

There, such murder rages through the days,
There, the earth became a sacred womb,
There, drunken laughter's gobbled by bayonets,

There, god blinded himself and became poor and naked,
One saw the wall wailing in sorrow,
Dead bodies lay sleeping on against their stone hearts.

THE PRISONER AND DEATH
(to my dear cellmate, Valtin Hartig)

The Prisoner says:

I think your name, Death, and it kills me.
The cell block in ruins, foundations laid bare;
The heavy iron rails rip themselves loose from their jambs
And warp in the maskless numb light.

My soul emits a cry. A shiver casts
 a frightened gesture
Into the blood, where the throbbing life is —
And how a mother strugglers for herself and her young,
So my blood grapples desperately for the source of the earth.

Oh, that I could flee! If you helplessly gave up
You're helplessly destroying yourself. Who gives up
Chooses you as a friend. But I want to live!

Ich will das Leben so, daß mich das Leben liebt
Und seinen Rhythmus durch mich strömt, mich Welterfüllten,
Deß trunkne Erdenlust nicht tausend Jahre stillten.
Der Tod spricht:

Da du das Leben willst, warum Erbleichen,
Wenn meine Melodie in deiner Seele tönt?
Wer mich erträgt, der atmet wie versöhnt,
Sein Herz kann nicht mehr greller Klang erreichen.

Ist tot der Baum im Herbst der Abendweiten?
Ist tot die Blume, deren Blüte fallend sich erfüllt?
Ist tot der schwarze Stein, der glutne Kräfte hüllt?
Ist tot die Erde über Gräbern menschlicher Gezeiten?

Oh, sie belogen dich! Auch ich bin Leben,
Ein Märchen sprachen sie: der Tod sei in der Welt.
Ich bin das Ewige im Spiel der Formen, die
Vollendung weben,

Dem Einen nahe, das den Sinn in Händen hält.
Ich bin der Wanderer, der überwand die tiefsten Wunden,
Und wer mich fand, der hat den Schoß der Welt gefunden.

PFADE ZUR WELT

Wir leben fremd den lauten Dingen,
Die um die Menge fiebernd kreisen,
Wir wandern in den stilleren Geleisen
Und lauschen dem Verborgnen, dem Geringen.

Wir sind dem letzten Regentropfen hingegeben,
Den Farbentupfen rundgeschliffner Kieselsteine,
Ein guter Blick des Wächters auslöscht das Gemeine,
Wir fühlen noch im rohen Worte brüderliches Leben.

Ein Grashalm offenbart des Kosmos reiche Fülle,
Die welke Blume rührt uns wie ein krankes Kind,
Der bunte Kot der Vögel ist nur eine Hülle

Des namenlosen Alls, dem wir verwoben sind.
Ein Wind weht menschlich Lachen aus der Ferne,
Und uns berauscht die hymnische Musik der Sterne.

I want life so, for life to love me
And as its rhythm streams through me — me, world-filled
By the drunken earthlust that hasn't slaked a thousand years.
Death speaks:

You that wants life so, why do you pale?
Is it because my melodies ring in your soul?
Who carries me breathes reconciliation
Whose heart can't hear such bright sound.

Is Death the tree in the autumn of the evening's distance?
Is Death the flower whose petals fall, realized?
Is Death the black stone that holds such power, radiating?
Is Death the earth above graves of human tides?

Oh, they've lied to you! I too am life,
From one of their fairy tales: "Death will be in the world,"
I am the Infinite in the game of forms, that which
weaves perfection,

The One draws closer who holds meaning in their hands.
I am the wanderer who's survived the deepest wounds,
And whoever finds me finds the womb of the world.

PATHS TO THE WORLD

We live outside the loud things
That circle feverish around the crowd,
We follow the quieter tracks
And listen in shadows to the little things.

We surrendered to the last raindrops,
To the darkened spots on smoothened pebbles,
A solid glance from the guard empties the commons,
We still feel fraternal life in raw words.

A blade of grass reveals the riches of the kosmos,
A wilting flower pulls on us like a sick child,
The colorful shit of the birds is only a shell

Of the nameless universe into which we're woven.
A wind blows human laughter from the distance,
And we are drunk on the hymnal music of the stars.

SCHWANGERES MÄDCHEN AUF DEM GEFÄNGNISHOF

Du schreitest wunderbar im Glast der mittaglichen Stunde,
Um deine Brüste rauscht der reife Wind,
Ein Lichtbach über deinen Nacken rinnt!
Oh, Hyazinthen blühen süß auf deinem Munde!

Du bist ein Wunderkelch der gnadenreichen
Empfängnis liebestrunkner Nacht,
Du bist von Lerchenliedern überdacht,
Und deine Last ist köstlich ohnegleichen.

Wer wird die Hand dir halten am verheißnen Tag,
Da Mutterwehen wimmern zitternde Spiralen?
Ich seh dein Auge, das vom rohen Wort erschrak,

Ich seh hinwelken deine Hüften in den fahlen
Jahren der Gefangenschaft. Ich seh die Wärterin, die ohne Scham
Das heimatlose Kind von deinen vollen Brüsten nahm

DÄMMERUNG

(Romain Rolland dankbar)

Am frühen Abend lischt das Leuchten deiner Zelle,
Von grauen Wänden gleiten schlanke Schatten,
Wer trotzig schrie, wird träumerisch ermatten,
Die braune Stille schwingt wie eine milde Welle.

Und oft erfüllt den engen Raum opalne Helle,
Gestalten deines Herzens locken dich zu heitrem Reigen,
Da wird ein Tanz im schweren Mantel Schweigen,
Da wird ein bunter Klang im dämmernden Gefälle.

Dein Atem ist ein Ruf, ein einziger Ruf!
Die Wächter schlürfen durch die Gänge, scheele Gäste.
Du bist so reich und lüdst sie ein zum Feste,

Das dir Genosse Abend schuf.
Doch grämlich drücken sie ans Guckloch trockne Schläfe …
Es ist kein Ruf, der ihre Herzen träfe.

A PREGNANT GIRL IN THE COMPOUND

You stride wonderfully through the glass of noon,
The ripening wind rushes round your breasts,
A stream of light runs over your neck!
Oh, hyacinth blooms sweet in your mouth!

You are a chalice of the
Conception of the lovedrunk night,
You are covered in lark song
And your weight is delicate beyond compare.

Who will hold your hand on the promised day
As your mothercries whine in quivering spirals?
I see your eye, horrified of the raw word,

I see your hips withering in those pale
Imprisoned years. I see the warden who,
 without shame,
Took the homeless child from your full breasts.

DUSK

(with thanks to Romain Rolland)

In early evening the glow of your cell dwindles,
Slender shadows slide from gray walls.
Should you scream, you'll tire dreamily.
The brown silence sinks like a soft wave.

And often an opal brightness fills the narrow space
And the shapes of your heart tempt you to dance:
There will be a dance in the heavy mantle of silence,
There will be an iridescent sound in the twilit gradient.

Your breath is a cry, a singular cry!
The guards slink along the corridors, jealous guests.
You are so rich and invite them to the feast

That brought you Comrade Evening.
But, brutally they press dry temples against the peep hole —
There is no cry that meets their hearts.

VERWEILEN UM MITTERNACHT

Um Mitternacht erwachst du. Glocken fallen
Wie Stürme an die Schwelle deines Traums.
Unendlich schwingt das Leben im Gefäß des Raums,
Ob allen Sternen muß sein Herzschlag hallen.

Es steigen an die Klänge, die sich ründen.
Die alte Stadt fühlt hilflos die gewordne Zeit,
Sie beugt sich tief: sie ist bereit,
In Schoß der Quelle einzumünden.

Hinschwingt ein letzter Klang in ferne Sphären.
Der Wandernde verweilt und lauscht:
Nur tiefer Stille wird Gebären,

Wer in der Erde wurzelt, rauscht.
Aus Stunden formt sich Antlitz gen die Zeiten
Und schwebt im Licht der Ewigkeiten.

NÄCHTE

Die Nächte bergen stilles Weinen,
Es pocht wie schüchtern Kindertritt an deine Wand,
Du lauschst erschreckt: Will jemand deine Hand?
Und weißt: Du reichst sie nur den Steinen.

Die Nächte bergen Trotz und Stöhnen,
Und wilde Sucht nach einer Frau,
Die Not des Blutes bleicht dich grau,
Aus Träumen blecken Fratzen, die dich höhnen.

Die Nächte bergen niegesungne Lieder,
In Nachttau blühn sie, samtne Schmetterlinge,
Sie küssen die verborgnen Dinge,

Du willst sie haschen und sie sind verweht,
Kein Weg ist, der zu ihnen geht.
Nie hörst du ihre Melodien wieder.

TO LINGER AT MIDNIGHT

You wake at midnight. Bells falling
Like thunder on the threshold of your dream.
Endlessly life flickers in the container of the room,
As if all the stars echo his heartbeat.

It rises to the sounds taking shape.
Helplessly the old town feels the turning time,
She bows deeply, she is ready
To enter the womb of the spring.

A final sound swinging into distant spheres.
The wanderer lingers and listens:
Only a deep silence will be born

Which, rooted in the earth, rustles.
From hours a face is formed against the times
And swims in the light of eternity.

NIGHTS

The nights carry silent crying.
It knocks like a frightened child's kicks on your wall.
You listen, terrified: Does someone want your hand?
And you know: you can only give it to the stones.

The nights carry defiance and moans
And a wild obsession with a woman,
The urgent blood bleaches you gray.
Dreams bare grimaces, scolding you.

The nights carry unsung songs,
Velvet butterflies, blooming in the night dew,
They kiss the buried things.

You want to catch them and they drift away.
There is no way that leads to them.
You never hear their melodies again.

NOVEMBER

Wie tote ausgebrannte Augen sind die schwarzen Fensterhöhlen
Im Dämmerabend der verhangenen Novembertage,
Wie Flüche wider Gott, hilflose Klage
Wider die Zwingherrn der verruchten Höhlen.

Die Städte sind sehr fern, darin die Menschen leben.
Ein Knäuel würgt die Kehle dir, ein Grauen
Betastet deine Glieder. Wer wird Freiheit schauen?
Wenn endlich wird sich dieses müde Sklavenvolk erheben?

Oh, niemand löscht die Stunden der Gefängnishöfe, die in wirren
Träumen uns gleich Fieberlarven schrecken, antlitzlosen,
Wir sind verdammt von Anbeginn, wir müssen wie Leprosen,

Unstete, durch die Jahre unsrer Jugend irren.
Was ist das Leben uns? Ein formlos farbenleer Verfließen...
Und gnädig sind die Nächte, die wie Särge uns umschließen.

EIN GEFANGENER REICHT DEM TOD DIE HAND

Erst hörte man den Schrei der armen Kreatur.
Dann poltern Flüche durch die aufgescheuchten Gänge,
Sirenen singen die Alarmgesänge,
In allen Zellen tickt die Totenuhr.

Was trieb dich, Freund, dem Tod die Hand zu reichen?
Das Wimmern der Gepeitschten? Die geschluchzten Hungerklagen?
Die Jahre, die wie Leichenratten unsern Leib zernagen?
Die ruhelosen Schritte, die zu unsern Häuptern schleichen?

Trieb dich der stumme Hohn der leidverfilzten Wände,
Der wie ein Nachtmahr unsre Brust bedrückt?
Wir wissen's nicht. Wir wissen nur, daß Menschenhände

Einander wehe tun. Daß keine Hilfebrücke überbrückt
Die Ströme Ich und Du. Daß wir den Weg verlieren
Im Dunkel dieses Hauses. Daß wir frieren.

NOVEMBER

Like dead, cauterized eyes are the black, gaping windows
In the twilight of dull November days,
Like curses against God, forsaken complaints
Against the landlords of loathsome lairs.

The cities are very far, where the people live.
You choke on a ball of wool, a horror
Touches your limbs. Who will be shown freedom?
When will this tired slave-people finally rise up?

Oh, nobody empties the prison hours, where in
Dreams we are all terrified by fever, faceless,
We are damned from the beginning, we must be leprosy,

Wandering unsteady through the years of our youth.
What is life to us? A formless, colorless flowing —
And merciful are the nights that embrace us like coffins.

A PRISONER REACHES A HAND TOWARD DEATH

First you hear the cry of that poor creature.
Then curses rumble through frightened halls,
Sirens sing the alarm-song, and
The deathwatch ticks in every cell.

What drove you, friend, to reach a hand toward Death?
The whimpers of the whipped? The swallowed pangs of hunger?
The years gnawing at our body like rats to a corpse?
The restless footsteps that slink into our heads?

Were you driven by the mute mockery of grief-ridden walls,
That push on our chest like a nightmare?
We do not know. We only know that human hands

Harm one another. That no bridge straddles
The rivers I and You. That we lose the way
In the dark of this house. That we are cold.

BESUCHER

Die Augen sind vom Haßschrei der Gefängnismauern
Verstört gleich Tauben, die ein Marder überfiel,
Und die verschüchtert flattern ohne Ziel,
Erblindet vor den Zähnen, die in Blutdurst lauern.

Dann Mitleid scheu erblüht wie blauer Klang der Harfen,
Die Herzen klammern sich an des Gefangnen Hand —
Oh, viele bittre Nächte weinten wie verbannt,
Seit Waffenknechte den Empörer ins Gefängnis warfen.

Der aber wuchs aus Last erstarrter Zellen,
Und seine Seele ward entrückt dem Rhythmus kleinen Lebens,
Er lebt nach innen, lebt an Gottes Quellen —

Und der Besucher friert und fühlt, er kam vergebens.
Ein Pilger, der den Weg zum Freund verloren ...
Und tiefer noch vereinsamt, weint er vor geschloßnen Toren.

GEMEINSAME HAFT

Sie sind gepfercht in einen schmalen Käfiggang,
Gleich Tieren, die an Gitterstäben wund sich biegen,
Und die von Heimweh krank am Boden liegen
Und fast erschrecken vor der eignen Stimme Klang.

Sie dorren hin und träge wird ihr Blut,
Nur böser Giftstrom bricht aus ihrem Munde,
Der sucht und ätzt des Nachbarn offne Wunde —
Die eingesperrten Menschen sind nicht gut.

Die eingesperrten Menschen sind gleich Kranken,
Sie wurden taub und stumm und blind,
Sie hassen sich, weil sie so ärmlich einsam sind.

Weil sie im Chaos ihres Ichs versanken,
Weil grobe Nähe auch des Freundes Antlitz roh und häßlich macht,
Weil jeder über jeden zu Gerichte sitzt und hämisch lacht.

VISITOR

Eyes disturbed by screams of hate from prison walls
Like pigeons attacked by a wolverine,
And the frightened birds flutter aimlessly,
Blinded by teeth lurking in bloodlust.

Then compassion blooms shy like the blue sound of harps,
Hearts cling to imprisoned hands —
Oh, many bitter nights weeping like exiles
Since the gunmen threw those rebels in prison.

But it grew from the burden of petrified cells
And his soul was enraptured by the rhythm of this little life,
He lives inside, lives at the sources of God —

And the visitor is cold and feels he came in vain.
A pilgrim who lost the way to a friend —
And deeper, lonelier again, he cries before closed gates.

COLLECTIVE CONFINEMENT

They are crammed in narrow cages
Like animals who bend raw against the bars,
And those who are homesick lie on the floor
Almost afraid of the sound of their voices.

They wither away and their blood grows slow,
Only a black stream of poison leaks from their mouths
Which searches for and etches into a neighbor's open wound —
The prisoners are not well.

The prisoners are all sick.
They grow deaf and mute and blind,
They hate themselves because they are so miserably alone.

Because they sank into the chaos of ego,
Because great proximity makes the face of a friend raw and ugly,
Because everyone tramples over everyone to sit and eat and gloat.

ENTLASSENE STRÄFLINGE

1918

(Meiner Mutter)

Sie träumen, Trunkne, durch vertraute Gassen,
Gefäß, darin ein Lichtmeer brandet,
In tausend Farben schäumt, im Asphalt strandet —
Form kann die Fülle noch nicht fassen.

Wie Auferstandne tasten sie mit durstgen Blicken
Nach Blätterknospen, die im Frühlingsatem schwellen …
Sie streifen von sich modrig Kleid verwester Zellen
Und wachsen flammend auf in irdischem Entzücken.

Doch Stadt erschreckt sie jäh wie fremdgespenstig Land …
Dann wieder sind sie tief in sich verklungen …
Unendlich fern die Zeit, da sie gebannt

In grauen Sarg, und hohle Wände Totenlied gesungen.
Zerbrechlich lächeln sie, als ob sie irgendwo Erloschnes fänden,
Und streichen fremdes Kind mit scheuen, unbeholfnen Händen.

UNSER WEG

Die Klöster sind verdorrt und haben ihren Sinn verloren,
Sirenen der Fabriken überschrillten Vesperklang,
Und der Millionen trotziger Befreiungssang
Verstummt nicht mehr vor klösterlichen Toren.

Wo sind die Mönche, die den Pochenden zur Antwort geben:
„Erlösung ist Askese weltenferner Stille …" —
Ein Hungerschrei, ein diamantner Wille
Wird an die Tore branden: „Gebt uns Leben!"

Wir foltern nicht die Leiber auf gezähnten Schragen,
Wir haben andern Weg zur Welt gefunden,
Uns sind nicht stammelndes Gebet die Stunden,

Das Reich des Friedens wollen wir zur Erde tragen,
Den Unterdrückten aller Länder Freiheit bringen —
Wir müssen um das Sakrament der Erde ringen!

DISCHARGED CONVICTS

1918

to my Mother

You, dreaming drunk through familiar alleys,
A sea of lights burns inside,
Foaming in a thousand colors against the asphalt —
Form cannot grasp this fullness.

How the resurrected grope around with thirsty sight
For leafbuds swelling in the spring's breath —
They strip themselves of their rotting dress
And grow up flaming in wordly delight.

But now cities terrify them like ghostly countries —
Then again they have sunk deep into themselves —
Infinitely distant is the time when they were paralyzed

In gray coffins, when hollow walls sang the deathsong.
They smile fragile smiles, as if they found something extinct,
And run their shy, clumsy hands over this new child.

OUR WAY

The monasteries have decayed and lost their meaning,
The sirens of factories screech over the vespers,
And the millions of defiant liberation songs
No longer fall silent on cloistered gates.

Where are the monks, who answer the throbbing:
"Salvation is the ascetic world-silence..." —
A joint cry of hunger, a single diamond will
Will burn into the gates: *Give us Life!*

We do not torment the bodies on the scaffold,
We have found another way to the world,
We are not stammering prayers for hours,

We want to bring the kingdom of peace to the earth,
To bring freedom to the oppressed of all countries,
We must struggle for the sacrament of the earth!

DAS SCHWALBENBUCH

THE BOOK OF SWALLOWS

Gewachsen 1922 • Geschrieben 1923
Festungsgefängnis
Niederschönenfeld

In meiner Zelle
nisteten im Jahre 1922
zwei Schwalben

Hatched 1922 • Written 1923
Correctional Facility
Niederschönenfeld

In 1922
Two swallows nest
In my cell

Ein Freund starb in der Nacht.
Allein.
Die Gitter hielten Totenwacht.

Bald kommt der Herbst.

Es brennt, es brennt ein tiefes Weh.

Verlassenheit.

A friend died in the Night.
Alone.
The iron bars hold a wake.

Autumn will come soon.

It burns, burns a deep sorrow:

Desolation.

O dumpfer Sang unendlicher Monotonie!
O ewiges Einerlei farblos zerrinnender Tage!
Immer
Wird ein Tag sein
Wie der letzte,
Wie der nächste,
Immer.

Zeit ist ein grauer Nebel. Der setzte sich in die Poren Deiner unendlichen Sehnsucht.

Das Stückchen blauer Himmel ist gespießt von rostigen Eisenstäben,
Die aus dem Gitterloch Deiner Zelle aufbrachen,
Auf Dich zuwanderten
Zu
Wanderten
Zu
Wanderten ...
Erst wehrtest Du Dich,

Aber die Gitterstäbe waren stärker als Du.
Nun wachsen Sie in Deinen Augen,
Und wohin Du blickst,
Überall
Überall siehst Du Gitterstäbe.
Noch das Kind, das im fernen, ach so fernen lupinenblühenden Feld spielt,
Ist gezwängt in die Gitterstäbe Deiner Augen.
Oh –

Deine Nächte, Deine Traumnächte verzweifelte Harlekinaden.

Deine Nägel kratzen am Sargdeckel tauber Verlassenheit.

Nirgends blüht das Wunder.

Musik ist

Wälder sind

Frauen sind

Oh, dull song of endless monotony!
Oh, eternal monotony of colorless days melting away!
Always
There will be a day
Like the last,
Like the next,
Always.

Time is a gray fog. It sits down in the pores of your boundless desire.

That piece of blue sky skewered by rusty iron bars
That burst through the opening in your cell,
Immigrating to you
Im-
Migrated
Im-
Migrated ...
First you struggled,

But the bars were stronger than you.
Now they're growing in your eyes,
And wherever you look,
Everywhere
Everywhere you see bars.
Even the child playing in the distant, oh so distant lupine-blooming field,
Is wedged in the iron of your eyes.
Oh —

Your nights, your dreamnights of desperate foolishness.

Your nails claw at the coffin of numb desolation.

The miracle blooms nowhere.

Music is

Forests are

Women are

Es blüht irgendwo die Geberde eines sanft
sich biegenden Nackens
Es wartet irgendwo eine Hand, die sehr
zärtlich ist und voll süßester Wärme

Nirgends blüht das Wunder.

Kalt wurde das Buch in meiner Hand,
So kalt, so kalt.
Die schwarzen Lettern schwarze Berge, die zu wandern begannen im Geäder meines Herzens.
Die raschelnden Blätter Schneefelder am Nordpol endloser Ohnmacht.

Ich friere.
Die Welt gerinnt.
Es muß schön sein einzuschlafen jetzt,
Kristall zu werden im zeitlosen Eismeer des Schweigens.
Genosse Tod.
Genosse, Genosse ...

Zirizi Zirizi Zirizi
Zizizi
Urrr

Daß man, nahe der dunklen Schwelle,
Solche Melodie vernimmt, so irdischen Jubels, so irdischer Klage trunken ...
Träume, meine Seele, träume,
Lerne träumen den Traum der Ewigkeit.

Zirizi Zirizi Zirizi
Zizizi
Urrr

It blooms somewhere: a soft gesture
of a bending neck.
Somewhere a hand is waiting, so tender,
full of the sweetest warmth.

The miracle blooms nowhere.

The book grows cold in my hands,
So cold, so cold.
The black letters black mountains that began to wander
from the veins of my heart.
The crackling leaves of snow-covered fields at
the north pole, endless frailty.

I am freezing.
The world curdles.
It must be nice, to drop into sleep,
To become crystal in this arctic sea of silence.
Comrade Death.
Comrade, Comrade ...

Zirizi Zirizi Zirizi
Zizizi
Urrr

That one, so near the dark threshold
Hears a melody, such mundane joy,
such earthly grievances ...
Dream, my soul, dream
Learn to dream the dream of eternity.

Zirizi Zirizi Zirizi
Zizizi
Urrr

Fort fort, Genosse Tod, fort fort,
Ein andermal, später, viel später.
Über mir über mir,
Auf dem Holzrahmen des halbgeöffneten Gitterfensters,
das in meine Zelle sich neigt in erstarrter
Steife, so als ob es sich betrunken hätte
und im Torkeln gebannt ward von einem
hypnotischen Blick,
Sitzt
Ein
Schwalbenpärchen.
Sitzt,
Wiegt sich! wiegt sich!
Tanzt! tanzt! tanzt!

Weichet zurück Ihr schwarzen Berge! Schmelzet Ihr Schneefelder!
Sonne Sonne, zerglühe sie! zerglühe sie!

Mütterliche!

Welche Landschaft wächst aus den verstaubten melancholischen
Zellenecken?
Tropische Felder, Farbenrausch sich entfaltender Orchideen!
Regina Noctis! –

Und darüber darüber
Mein Schwalbenpaar.
Das Wunder ist da!
Das Wunder!
Das Wunder!

Tanze meine atmende Brust,
Tanzet Ihr wunden geketteten Augen,
Tanzet! Tanzet!
Nur im Tanze brecht Ihr die Fessel,
Nur im Tanze umrauscht Ihr die Sterne,
Nur im Tanze ruht Ihr im Göttlichen,
Tanzet! Tanzet!

Im Tanze träumt das heilige Lied der Welt.

Away, away, Comrade Death, go, go
Another time, later, much later.
Above me, around me
On the wooden frame of the half-opened barred window
that slants in my cell, petrified,
as if it had been drunk and
staggering and spellbound by a
hypnotic gaze,
Sits
A
Pair of swallows,
Sits,
Swaying, swaying!
Dance! dance! dance!

Sink back into your black mountains, melt your fields of snow,
The sun, sun tore them, burnt them apart.

Maternal!

What landscape rises from the melancholic dust of
these cells?
Tropical fields, colordrunk unfolding orchids!
Regina Noctis! —

And above above
My swallows.
The miracle is here!
The miracle!
Miracle!

Dance my breathing breast,
Dance your sore, chained eyes,
Dance! Dance!
Only in the dance your bondage breaks
Only in the dance do you smoke the stars,
Only in the dance do you rest in the divine,
Dance! Dance!

In the dance, the sacred song of the world is dreaming.

Von den Ufern des Senegal, vom See Omandaba
Kommt Ihr, meine Schwalben,
Von Afrikas heiliger Landschaft.
Was trieb Euch zum kalten April des kalten Deutschland?
Auf den griechischen Inseln habt Ihr gerastet,
Sangen nicht heitere Kinder Euch heiteren Gruß?
Warum nicht bautet Ihr Tempel in des Archipelagos
Ehrwürdigen Locken?

Zu welchem Schicksal kamet Ihr?

O unser Frühling
Ist nicht mehr Hölderlins Frühling,
Deutschlands Frühling ward wie sein Winter,
Frostig und trübe
Und bar der wärmenden
Liebe.

Den Dichtern gleichet Ihr, meine Schwalben.

Leidend am Menschen, lieben sie ihn mit nie erlöschender
Inbrunst,
Sie, die den Sternen, den Steinen, den Stürmen tiefer verbrüdert
sind als jeglicher Menschheit.
Den Dichtern gleichet Ihr, meine Schwalben.

Wo soll ich Euch eine Stätte bereiten, Vögel der Freiheit?
Ich bin ein Gefangener, und mein Wille ist nicht mein Wille.
Sing ich ein Lied der Freiheit, meldet der Wächter:
Der Gefangene sang ein revolutionäres Lied.
Das dulden die Paragraphen nicht.
Mächtige Herren sind die Paragraphen, die die Menschen über
sich setzten, weil sie den Sinn verloren. Ruten tragen sie in Händen. Die
Menschen sagen: Ruten der Gerechtigkeit.
Dieses Hauses Ruten heißen: Einzelhaft Bettentzug Kostentzug
Hofverbot Schreibverbot Sprechverbot Singverbot Leseverbot
Lichtverbot Zwangsjacke.

Ihr, meine Schwalben, wißt nichts von Gerechtigkeit und nichts
von Ungerechtigkeit. Darum wißt Ihr auch nichts von
Paragraphen und von Ruten ...

From the shores of Senegal, from Lake Omandaba
They come, my swallows,
From Africa's sacred landscape.
Why do they fly to this cold April of this cold Germany?
On the Greek isles they rested,
Did cheerful children not sing you cheerful greetings?
Why did they not build a temple on the archipelago's
venerable saplings?

Which fate have you come to?

Oh, our spring
Is no longer Hölderlin's spring,
Germany's spring just like it's winter,
Frosty and gray
Deprived of the warming
Love.

You sail to the poets, my swallows.

Suffering humanity; love them with never-ending
fervor,
They who are deeper friends with the stars, the stones, the storms
than any humanity.
My swallows, you sail to the poets.

Where should I prepare a nest for you, birds of freedom?
I am a prisoner, and my will is not my will.
I sing a song of freedom. The warden reports:
This prisoner sang a song of revolution.
Our paragraphs do not tolerate that.
Powerful men find the paragraphs that people skipped because they lost their
meaning. They interrogate with their hands. The people call for justice. The cries
of this house mean: Solitary confinement — No beds
— Hope, forbidden — Cries, forbidden — Speech, forbidden — Song, forbidden
— Books, forbidden — Light, forbidden —
— Straightjacket.

You, my swallows, know nothing of justice and nothing
of injustice. Therefore you know nothing of
paragraphs and screams —

Wie soll ich Euch ein Bettchen holen?
Wohl ist das Haus, das mir die Menschen als Wohnung wiesen, bajonettbehütet und stacheldrahtumwehrt. Wohl hallen Tag und Nacht die Höfe von des Wächters ruhelosen Schritten. Aber die Rutenträger sagen, ein Stückchen Holz sei gefährlich.

Gefährlich der Ordnung und Ruhe und Sicherheit des Hauses.

Hilfreicher Freund!
Ein Stückchen Pappe halfest du mir über die Zellentür fugen.

O bleibt Gefährten mir, Schwalben!

Die lockende Bucht umflattern
Ängstlich die Schwalben.
Eine berührt sie.
Das Männchen!
Schon kenn ichs
Am länger sich pfeilenden
Schwanz, am roten
Spitzigen Brustmal.
Jäh erschrickt es.
Fliegt davon.
Das Weibchen schrill schreiend
Mit ihm.

Ahntet Ihr,
Wohin ich Euch locken wollte?

Ach wer sollte freiwillig
Einkehren in eine
Gefangenenzelle?

How could I build you a crib?
This house is good that the people have shown me:
guarded by bayonets and barbed wire. Day and Night echo
the watchmen's restless footsteps through the fields.
Even the beams say a piece of wood is dangerous.

Dangerous to the order and peace and security of the house.

Helpful friend!
You helped me put a piece of cardboard over the cell door.

Oh stay, my companions, my swallows!

The swallows flutter anxious
Around the tempting bay.
One touches the other.
The male!
Already I recognize
The long forked tail,
The red,
Pointed breast.
Suddenly startled.
Flying away.
The female's shrill cries
With him.

Could you tell
Where I wanted to lure you?

Ah, who would willingly
Enter a
Prison cell?

Sechs Schritt hin
Sechs Schritt her

Ohne Sinn

Ohne Sinn

Six steps there
Six steps back

Without sense

Without sense

Die Schwalben sind zurückgekehrt.

Sie bleiben! Sie bleiben!

Nach Osten blickt meine Zelle.

Nach Osten!

The swallows have come back.

They stay! They stay!

My cell faces the east.

The east!

O Europa, wie arm Du bist!
Die Tiere Deiner Häuser sind wie Deine Menschen,
Geduckt und häßlich, verkrüppelt und verschnitten.
O ihre traurigen Augen!
Wo Du sie krönst, krönst Du Rekorde.
Wie Du Deiner Menschen Rekorde krönst –
Und nicht ihr Leben! Und nicht ihr Leben!

Wann wachsen sie ihr Leben?
Wann?
Sie übergeben es einem Götzen, der eine Uniformmütze trägt, der ordnet es, katalogisiert es, befiehlt Pflichten, schreibt Geburtsscheine, Militärscheine, Trauscheine, Sterbescheine, setzt ein Kreuz hinter ihre abgespulten Namen, trägt den vollgeschriebenen Registerband in die Registratur, So muß es sein, So dienst Du Gott,
In Ewigkeit, Amen.

Brecht auf Ihr Völker des Orients und
verkündet die seligen Hymnen eurer Gebenedeiten Muße!!!

Ein Tier aber lebt in Euren Häusern, Ihr Menschen Europas, das ließ sich nicht zähmen und züchten,
Das ließ sich nicht fangen von Eurer süßlichen Lockung und Eurer herrischen Drohung,
Das blieb
Frei!
Frei!
Frei!

Kommt zu mir dem zwiefach Gefangenen:
Gefangener eingekerkert von Gefangenen ...

In dieser Nacht
Schlief das Schwalbenpärchen in meiner Zelle.

Oh Europe, how poor you are!
The animals of your houses are like your people,
Crouched and ugly, crippled and bent.
Oh the sadness in your eyes!
Where you crown them, you write the records.
How you write your people's records —
And not their lives! And not their lives!

When will they rise to their lives?
When?
They surrender their records to an idol who wears a uniform, who organizes them, catalogs them, orders duties, writes birth certificates, military notes, marriage certificates, death certificates, places a cross behind their unwound names, carries the complete register, As it must be, As one serves god,
For ever and ever, Amen.

Rise you heralds of the East, and
deliver the hymns of your blessed stillness!!!

But an animal lives in your houses, you people of Europe, that cannot be tamed or captured,
could not be caught by your temptations or your
imperial threats,
It remains
Free!
Free!
Free!

Come to me you prisoners:
Prisoners imprisoned by prisoners ...

On this night
The swallows sleep in my cell.

Baumeister gotischer Kathedrale,
Zügle den Stolz!
Quadern brauchtest Du und kunstvoll gemeißelte Steine,
Pfeiler, Pilaster, Rosetten und farbige Scheiben,
Mörtel war Dir
Das Elend der Menge, das billig sich feilbot,
Weihtest Dein Werk
Dem Jenseits,
Dem Tode.

Siehe die Schwalben:

Aus Schmutz, aus Schlamm, aus Halmen, aus Haaren der
Pferde
Bauen sie fromm ihr edel gewölbtes Nest,
Weihens
Der Erde,
Dem Leben.

Am Morgen, wenn der Wächter kommt,
Schreck ich zusammen.
Entdeckt er das Nest,
Reißt ers mit harter Geberde zu Boden.

O im vorigen Sommer der Kriegszug auf junges Getier!
Gegen Dachrinnen, Firste marschierte man Sturm.
Als ich zum Hof ging,
Ging ich über ein Schlachtfeld.

Hilflos kreisend die klagenden Mütter.

Paragraph X: Es widerspricht dem Strafvollzug,
Vögel zu dulden im Hause der Buße.

Menschen Menschen

Architects of gothic cathedrals,
Curb your pride!
You'll need cubes and ornately chiseled stones,
Columns, pilasters, rosettes amd colorful panels
You were the mortar,
The blend of the masses offered itself,
Consecrates your work
To the hereafter,
To Death.

See the swallows:

From squalor, from sludge, out of stalks, out of the hairs
of horses
They build their hallowed nest,
Consecrated in the name of
The Earth,
Of Life.

When the watchman comes in the morning
I tremble all over.
He discovers the nest, and
In one rough gesture, knocks to the ground.

Oh last summer the campaign against young animals!
Against the rain, roofs marching against the storm.
As I went to the field
I went over a battlefield.

The wailing mothers circle helplessly.

Paragraph X: It contradicts the prison system
to excuse birds of their fines.

People People

Ich sah Schmetterlinge spielen
Im sonneflirrenden Mittag.

Wo aber,
Wenn die Sonne sinkt,
Wenn Nachtstürme
Über die Erde rauschen
Mit schwarzem Gefieder,
Wo, lieblichste Kinder der göttlichen Mutter,
Schlafet Ihr dann?

Ich glaube,
Es öffnen sich Euch
Die Kelche der Blumen,
Ich glaube,
Es wiegt Euch zur Ruhe
Der Blütenklang im Dom der Kastanien.

I saw butterflies playing
In the shimmering noon.

But where,
When the sun sinks,
When the nightstorms
Rush over the earth
With black feathers,
Where, lovely children of the divine mother,
Shall you sleep then?

I think
It will open for you,
Goblets of flowers
I think
It will lull you to sleep:
The bleeding sound in the shell of a chestnut.

Im Nest,
Gebettet in weiße daunige Federn,
Liegen
Fünf braungesprenkelte Eier.

Fünf festliche Tempel keimenden Lebens.

In the nest
Bedded in white featherdown
Lay
Five brown-speckled eggs.

Five festive temples of budding life.

Die Menschenmütter,
Ach sie sind nicht mehr
Festliche Tempel keimenden Lebens.

In meiner Mutter Hände
Kerben sich Runzeln.
Als sie mich trug,
War ihr Blut
Beschattet von täglicher Not.
Träumend
Wuchs ich
Im Dunkel des wärmenden Schoßes ...
Meine Milch Schwermut.
Mein Herzschlag Trauer.

Das Lied in Moll
Wahre der Mensch
Im hymnischen Chor der Welt.

The people's mothers,
Oh, they're no longer
Festive temples of budding life.

In my mother's hands
Scars frown
As they carry me,
Her blood was
Shadowed by daily necessity.
Dreaming
I woke
In the dark, warm womb ...
Milk's melancholy.
The mourning beat of my heart.

A song in minor
Truth of man
In the hymnal choir of the world.

Weißt Du, wie eine Schwalbe fliegt?

Ich sah
Im Kriege Gefangene wandern
Durch klagende Täler zerschossener Dörfer.
Den Reihen der Gaffenden
Entkrümmte sich
Ein Weib.
Hände gekrampft lösten sich,
Stiegen steil in Äther schwärzlichen Himmels,
Stiegen! Stiegen!
Schwebten!
Jauchzten!
Und einer Stimme seraphischer Jubel:
André!!!

Aber es war nicht wie der Flug einer Schwalbe.

Ich sah
Im Gefängnis gefesselte Menschen
Schlafend ...
Träumend ...
O Antlitz sternenstrahlend!
Gefesselte Menschen
Träumend!
Du seliger Sieger Traum!!!

Aber es war nicht wie der Flug einer Schwalbe.
Der Schwalbe Flug – wie Unnennbares nennen?
Der Schwalbe Flug – wie Unbildbares bilden?
Lebte ein Gott,
Sein Zorn:
Der Schwalbe schnellendes Pfeilen,
Sein Lächeln:
Der Schwalbe innigweises Spiel,
Seine Liebe:
Der Schwalbe trunknes Sichverschenken.

Europa preist seine Äroplane,
Ich aber, ich Nummer 44,
Will mit den schweigenden Akkorden meines Herzens
Den Flug der Schwalbe preisen.

Wer preist mit mir den Flug der Schwalbe?

Do you know how a swallow flies?

I saw
Prisoners wandering through the war
Through wailing valleys and shattered villages.
Rows of dimmed streets.
A woman
Unwinds
Cramped hands, detached
And climbing high into the black ether,
Climbing, climbing,
Floating,
Exulting.
And in a single voice of seraphic joy, cries:
André!!!

But it was not like the flight of a swallow.

I saw
People bound in prison
Sleeping...
Dreaming...
Oh, starbright face!
Prisoners
Dreaming
Happy dreams of victory.

But it was not like the flight of a swallow.
How does one name the unnameable?
How to imagine the unimaginable?
There lived a god —
His anger:
the swallow's quick arrows,
His laugh:
the swallow's intimate game,
His love:
drunk, the swallow itself a gift.

Europe praises its airplanes,
But I — number 44 —
With the sinking chords of my heart,
Want to praise the flight of the swallow.

Who else praises the swallow's flight?

Alle lade ich ein!
Wer kommt?

Ein ältliches Mädchen.
Ein buckliges Kind.
Ein Narr.

O lächerliche Trinität menschlicher Güte!

Wir preisen! Amen.
Wir singen! Amen.
Wir beten an! Amen.

Wir preisen den Flug der Schwalbe,
Aber so heißt ihres Fluges Offenbarung:

Das Tier ist heiliger als der Mensch. Amen.
Die Blume heiliger als das Tier. Amen.
Erde heiliger als die Blume. Amen.
Aber am heiligsten der Stein. Sela. Sela. Sela.

I invite you all.
Who answers?

An elderly girl.
A hunchbacked child.
A fool.

Oh, you absurd trinity of mortal gods,

We praise! Amen.
We sing! Amen.
We worship! Amen.

We worship the flight of the swallow,
But the name of her flight — revelation!

The animal is more sacred than man. Amen.
The flower is more sacred than animal. Amen.
The earth is more sacred than flower. Amen.
But the most sacred is the stone. Selah. Selah. Selah

Morgens putzt sich das Schwalbenmännchen
Mit feiner Grazie
Sein bläulich blitzendes Gefieder.
Immer ist die Schwälbin unzufrieden,
Schilt ihn, zankt ihn, plappert, poltert
Ein scheckiges Kauderwelsch.
Würdig beendet das Männchen
Seine Morgenfrisur,
Antwortet kaum den keifenden Lauten.
Dann – heidi!
Fliegts in die tauigen Himmel.
Aber nicht lange,
Sitzts auf dem Fensterrahmen,
Zwitschert der brütenden Gattin
Ein fröhliches Morgenkonzert.
Zirizi, Zirizi,
Zizizi,
Urrr.

Mornings, gracefully,
The male grooms
His bluish, gleaming plumage.
The woman is never satisfied.
She scolds him, babbles, prattles
A dappled gibberish.
He hardly answers her.
Then — flies
into the dewy sky.
But not for long,
There, on the window frame,
Chirps the brooding wife,
A joyous concert for the morning.
Zirizi, Zirizi,
Zizizi,
Urrr.

Ich stehe am nächtlichen Gitterfenster.

Träumend zwitschert die Schwälbin.
Geweckt vom liebenden Ruf
Regt sich leise das Schwalbenmännchen.

Ich bin nicht allein.

Auch Mond und Sterne sind mir Gefährten
Und die schimmernden schweigenden Felder.

At night I stand at the barred windows.

The female chirps as she dreams.
The male softly stirs,
Woken by the loving call.

I am not alone.

The moon and stars are my companions.
And the shimmering, silent fields.

Menschen wie arm Eure Feste!
Jazztänze schrill von verruchter Zeit!
Eure Lebensangst
Ankurbelt die Autos der Selbstflucht,
Illuminiert
Die Seele
Mit Lampions elektrischer Gier
Und wähnt:
Sie sei geborgen.

Aber sie ist geborgen nicht

All Euer Lärm, Euer Gekreisch, Euer Gekrächz,
Euer Freude plakatieren, Lustig sind wir:
Hahaha –
Übertönt nicht
Das leise kratzende
Nagen
Der drei heimlichen Ratten
Leere   Furcht   Verlassenheit

Aber schon schaue ich Dich,
Gewandelte Jugend der Revolution.

Deine Tat: Zeugung.
Deine Stille: Empfängnis.
Dein Fest: Geburt.
Opfernd
Im todnahen Kampfe heroischer Fahnen

Schreitend
Im reifenden Felde träumenden Frühlings,
Jauchzend
Im bindenden Tanze gelöster Leiber,
Ahnend
Im magischen Schweigen gestirnter Nacht.

Schon schaue ich Dich,
Gewandelte Jugend der Revolution.

Your parties are lacking, people!
Jazz dances, shrill from loathsome time!
Your fear of life
Starts the engine in the cars of escapism,
Illuminates
The soul
With lanterns of electric greed
And you think
You are safe.

But you are not safe.

All your noise, your screeching, your croaking,
your pleasure, happygolucky:
Hahaha —
Nothing drowns out
The soft scratching
Gnawing
Of the three holy rats
Emptiness Fear Desolation

But already I look at you
Transformed youth of the Revolution.

Your task: Procreation
Your silence: Conception
Your celebration: Birth
Sacrificed
In the deathnear struggles of heroic flags

Screaming,
Dreaming of spring in ripening fields,
Rejoicing
Bodies dissolved in the binding dance,
Waking
in the deep silence of night.

Already I am looking at you
Transformed youth of the Revolution.

Ihr meine brüderlichen, Ihr meine tapferen Schwalben!
Auf dem Hofe steh ich.
In morgenlichen Lüften segelt, spreitend die mächtigen
Flügel mit Würde, ein Sperber.
Ich höre gelle Schreie spielender Schwalben.
Von allen Seiten antworten Rufe.
Scharen von Schwalben fliegen herbei.
Wer gab das Angriffssignal?
In gepfeilter Wucht stürzen sie auf den königlichen Vogel,
Der in seinen Fängen einen jungen Sperling krallt.
Ihr meine brüderlichen, Ihr meine tapferen Schwalben!
Doch welch ungleicher Kampf!
Gelassen, mit bewegterem Flügelschlag, wehrt der Angegriffene.
Kaum achtet er der winzigen Verfolger.
Armer Sperling!
Immer wieder greifen die Schwalben den Räuber an.
Bedrängen ihn mit feuriger Leidenschaft.
Schon werden seine Flügelschläge hastiger, unbeherrschter ...
Die Schwachen haben den Starken besiegt!!
Zornigen Schreis, bezwungen von verbündeter Kraft öffnet der Sperber die kerkernden Fänge.
Zitternd entflattert der betäubte Spatz.
In seligen Flügen feiern die Schwalben den Sieg der Gemeinschaft.

You my brothers, you my brave swallows!
I stand in the yard.
In the morning air, on mighty
wings of grandeur, sails a sparrowhawk.
I hear the screams of swallows playing.
The calls are answered from all sides.
Flocks of swallows flying by.
Who gave the signal?
As a single arrow they rush toward the royal bird,
Who holds a young sparrow in his talons.
You my brothers, you my brave swallows!
It was no contest.
Unperturbed, with a single beat of his wing,
the sparrowhawk deflects the attack.
Poor sparrow!
He hardly pays attention to his pursuers.
Again and again the swallows attack the thief.
They press him with firey passion,
Already his wings beat faster, unrestrained...
The weak have conquered the strong!!
Cries of wrath, defeated by a joint power,
 opens the prison of his talons.
Shaking, the stunned sparrow flutters.
On blessed winds the swallows celebrate this victory of communion.

Wann endlich, Tiere, bündet Ihr Euch
Zum Bunde wider die Menschheit?
Ich, ein Mensch,
Rufe Euch auf!
Euch Nachtigallen, geblendet mit glühender Nadel,
Euch Hammel, gewürgt in Kasematten vergaster Übungsschiffe,
Euch Esel, sanfteste Tiere, zusammenbrechend unter Peitschenhieben,
Euch Strauße, zuckenden Atems gerupft und fühlenden Herzens,
Euch Pferde, sonnenlos werkend in verpesteten Schächten,
Euch Bären, dressiert auf glühender Eisenmatte,
Euch Löwen, gezähmt im Zirkus von stählerner Knute,
Euch Alle   Euch Alle
Rufe ich auf!
Erwachet!
Rächen wollen wir
Die Opfer des Menschen:
Tiere für Gaumenkitzel atmend gefoltert,
Tiere für Modelaunen lachend geschunden,
Tiere berauschten Arenen eitel geopfert,
Tiere in Kriegen sinnlos zerfetzt ...

Ich will mich an Eure Spitze stellen,
Ich, ein Renegat der Menschheit,
Will Euch führen gegen den einen Feind
Mensch.

Tiere der Wüste: Brüllet Alarm!
Tiere des Dschungels: Heulet Sturm!

Keine Unterscheidung lassen wir gelten.
Weiße und Schwarze, Gelbe und Braune,
Alle alle Erdschänder! Muttermörder! Sternenräuber!
Auf dem gebuckelten Nestrand
Sitzt die Schwälbin.
Schaut mit ernsten, erwartenden Augen
(Wie wenig kennen die Menschen
Eure Augen, Tiere!)
Auf die heilige Stätte der Wandlung.
Ab und zu
Klopft sie mit knackendem Schnabel
An kalkumpanzerte Welten

When will you animals form
a union against mankind?
I, a man,
Call you to this.
You nightingales, dazzled by bright needles,
You rams, strangled to the casemates, gassed on barges,
You donkeys, the gentlest animals, collapsing under lashes,
You ostriches, your twitching breath and feeling hearts plucked away,
You horses, sunless, toiling in polluted mineshafts,
You bears, trained on glowing iron mats,
You lions, tamed in the circus by a steel knucle,
All of you   all of you
I call!
Awaken!
We want revenge
Human sacrifices:
Animals choking so you can taste them,
Animals laying flayed on the whim of fashion,
Animals killed in vain for your drunken games,
Animals torn to shreds in senseless wars ...

I want to put myself in your stead
I, a renegade of humanity,
Will lead you against your one enemy
Man.

Desert animals: roar the alarm!
Jungle animals: howl the storm!

There is no distinction among us.
White and black, yellow and brown,
All, all descrators of the Earth!! Matricide! Star-thief!
Hunched at the edge of the nest
The swallow sits.
Looks with serious, expectant eyes
(How little do people know
Your eyes)
At the holy place of change.
Now and then
She knocks with a clicking beak
On calcified worlds

Trächtigen Lebens.
Lauschend verweilt sie

Unsäglich zärtlicher Laut!
Eilig fliegt das Männchen herbei,
Aufgeregt, geschäftig, betriebsam
Umkreist es plaudernd das Nest.
Gleich in schelmischer Freude
Wehrt die Schwälbin
Dem forschenden Flug.
Endlich hält sie inne.
Sehr sanft wird ihr Blick,
Sehr weich und gelöst
Ihre Geberde.

Und das Schwalbenmännchen
Erschaut
Sich,
Sich in fünf winzigen
Blinden, atmenden
Gesichten.
Laßt mich teilnehmen
An Eurer Beglückung,
Gefährten.
Pate will ich den fünfen sein,
Mitsorgender, helfender Schützer.

Ich gratuliere! Ich gratuliere!

Pregnant with life.
She lingers, listening

Unspeakably gentle sound!
The little man flies over quickly,
Excited, industrious, busy
He circles the nest chatting.
Equally mischievous
She resist's the swallow's
Curious flight.
Finally she pauses.
Her gaze becomes very gentle,
Very soft and relaxed,
She gestures.

And the male swallow
He sees
Himself,
In five tiny
Blind, breathing
Faces.
Let me take part
In your joy,
Companions.
I want to be their godfather
Caring, helpful protector.

I congratulate you!

Schwälbchen, der Morgen, der Morgen ist da!
Nachts hat Mutter Euch Märchen gezwitschert,
Jetzt sucht sie Brot zum Schnäbleinstopfen,
Schwälbchen, der Morgen, der Morgen ist da.

Schwälbchen, der Morgen, der Morgen ist da!
Sonne pocht an und will Euch begrüßen,
Öffnet die braunen Guckäugelein,
Schwälbchen, der Morgen, der Morgen ist da.

Schwälbchen, der Morgen, der Morgen ist da!
Bald seid Ihr groß, dann werdet Ihr fliegen
Fort übers Meer zu den Negerlein,
Schwälbchen, der Morgen, der Morgen ist da.

Swallows, the morning, the morning is here!
All night your mother whispered fairy tales
Now shes on the hunt to stuff your little beaks,
Oh swallow the morning, the morning is here!

Swallows, the morning, the morning is here!
The knocking of the sun says it wants to meet you
Softly open your little brown eyes,
Oh swallow the morning, the morning is here!

Swallows, the morning, the morning is here!
Soon you'll be big enough to fly away
Far across the sea where little Indians play,
Oh swallow the morning, the morning is here.

Graue seidene Härchen
Wachsen in komischen Büscheln
Aus rosigen Leibern.
Aufgespießt auf einem dünnen
Überlangen Hals
Der Kopf ...
Reißt eins das gelbe Schnäbelchen auf,
Bleckt
Ein lächerlich wütender Rachen.

Immer bleibt das Nest sauber.
Liegt drin ein weißes Würstchen
Mit schwarzem geringeltem Schwänzchen,
Wirds von den Eltern gepackt
Und hinausgetragen.

Eifrig füttern sie
Das junge Getier.
Erst wird das Futter
Im Kropf erweicht,
Mit Speichel zart bereitet,
Dann in die hungrigen Mäuler gestopft.
Hat der Vater
Das Junge zur Rechten gefüttert,
Füttert die Mutter
Das Junge zur Linken.
Geheimes Gesetz
Waltet.

Wie ein Kind, das am Bilde sich freut, am Spiele
Holderer Wesen,
Sah ich Dir zu.
Nun seh ich ein wissender Mensch.

Was trägst Du,
Gewürgt vom krallenden Schnabel,
Den hungrigen Jungen herbei?
Ein Tierchen gleich Dir,
Deine kleine Schwester Fliege.
Verkettet auch Du der Urschuld des Lebens!
Weh uns!
Was lebt, mordet.

Silky gray hairs
Pop up in strange clusters
On rosy bodies.
Impaled on a long
Outstretched neck,
The head —
A yellow beak tears,
Bares
An absurd, blazing pharynx.

The nest is always kept clean.
A small saussauge lies there
With a black-ringed tail,
The parents grab it
And carry it out.

Eagerly they feed
Their young.
First softened
In her craw,
Delicately seasoned with saliva,
Then stuffed into hungry mouths.
The father
feeds the one on the right,
The mother,
those on the left.
An unspoken law
Prevails.

Like a child who delights in pictures, at the games
Of gentler beings,
I watched you.
Now I see a wiser man.

What do you carry,
Trapped in your beak,
To the hungry boy?
A little creature like you,
A small fly, your sister.
You too, shackled to the sin.
Woe to us.
What lives, murders.

Ich will Dich lieben mit tieferer Liebe,
Da ich weiß, was Schicksal Dich tun heißt.

Es ist ein Fluch der Erde,
Nirgends
Atmet das Lebendige
In göttlicher Unschuld.
Und noch das Tote
Muß töten.

I want to love you with a deeper love,
Since I know what fate will to do with you.

It's a curse of earth.
Nowhere
In divine innocence
Breathe the living.
Even the dead
Must kill.

Ei, Schwälbchen,
Was Du nicht kannst!

Zaghaft und mutig doch
Steigt eins
Auf die Borden des Nestes,
Hebt zierlich sein Schwänzchen ...
Klacks!
Hats sein Werk vollbracht,
Putzt sich
Den kleinen Popo
Mit gesträubten Flügeln,
Und eilig, erhobenen Kopfes,
Stolz wie ein Russenzar
Kriechts in sein Nest zurück.

Egg, little swallow,
What can't you do!

One climbs,
Cautious, yet courageous
To the corner of the nest,
Carefully lifts its tail
Floop!
Now his work is done,
He wipes
His little bottom
With bristled wings
And hurried, head held high,
Proud as a Russian Tsar
Slips back into his nest.

Sah schreiten ein Mädchen
Im Weizenfeld.
Leuchtet ihr rotes Tuch,
Rotes Tuch, rotes Tuch
Oder ihr Herz

Sang fern eine Drossel
Im Fliederbusch.
Klang wie ein Liebeslied,
Liebeslied, Liebeslied
Oder auch Spott

Ein Sommer noch,
Zwei Sommer noch,
Trallalala, Trallalala

Saw a girl walking
In a field of wheat.
Her red scarf flashes
Red scarf red scarf
Or her heart

Sang a thrush far
In the lilacs.
Rang like a lovesong
Lovesong lovesong
Or sarcasm

One more summer,
Two more summers,
Trallalala, Trallalala

Drohte Gefahr, klagen würde die Schwälbin
Mit schrillem Pfeifen
Den Winden ihre dumpfe Angst.
Vom Fenster zum Nest, vom Nest zum Fenster
Fliegt sie gelassen.
Im Neste hocken,
Eins sich kauernd ans andere,
Die Jungen.
Über den Nestrand
Lugen die Köpfe,
Beugen sich vor, ducken zurück, wiegen sich rhythmisch
Im Takte mütterlichen Flugs.
Streichen der Schwälbin Flügel
Das wärmende Nest,
Recken sie schreiende Schnäbel,
Zärtlicher Wartung gewöhnt.
Aber gleich in ernstem Besinnen
Verstummen sie,
Und in kindlichen Augen wird wach
Ein seltsames Leuchten.

Lockende Laute zwitschert die Schwälbin,
Verweilend.

The mother, alert,
Whistles her fear
Into the wind.
Cooly, she bounces
Window to nest, nest to window.
Crouching in the nest,
The young
huddled together.
Over the edge of the nest
Peep their heads,
Bending forward, ducking back, rocking rhythmically
To the pulse of the mother's flight.
Stretching her wings
To warm the nest,
A chorus of screeching beaks resounds,
Accustomed to this tender service.
But suddenly in deep reflection
They fall silent;
A strange glow wakes
In childish eyes.

Their mother calmly coos
All the while.

O köstliches Wunder!
Krabbelt ein Junges hervor,
Spreitet die winzigen Flügel ...
Erhebt sich ...
Fliegt,
Fliegt
Schwankend und dennoch voll Anmut,
Leiht seiner Angst
Die zierliche Geste edler Gesittung,
Setzt sich, klopfenden Herzens,
Neben die glückliche Mutter.

Mit Lob und leckeren Bissen
Verwöhnen die Eltern
Das mutige Junge.

Die im Neste
Erheben Geschimpf und Geschelt.

Auf den nahen Dachfirst fliegt das tapfere Junge.
Neugierig beguckts die Welt.
Beguckt zum erstenmal die Welt.
Freunde, ich sehe mit ihm zum erstenmal die Welt.
Da sitzt mein Schwälbchen. Über sich die leuchtende,
Wärmende Sonne, unter sich die blühende, atmende Erde.
Die Blumen, die Bäume, die Dachziegel,
Die fernen Wälder, die Telegraphendrähte,
Alle alle beugten grüßend
Die schweigenden Häupter.

Es rauschen die reifenden Ähren
Auch mir dem Gefangenen.
Es wölbt sich des Sommers blauender Himmel
Auch diesem gestorbenen Hof.
Ich atme
Im Mittag süßer Beglückung.

Erde! Geliebte!

O precious miracle!
A hatchling crawls out,
Spreads its tiny wings ...
Rises,
Flies,
Flies
Wavering graceful,
His fear
Lends an air of delicate nobility.
He sits, beating heart,
Next to his proud mother.

With praise and delicious food
The parents spoil
Their brave son.

Those in the nest
Howl and scold.

The courageous youth flies to a ridge nearby.
He looks out at the curious world.
Looks, for the first time, at the world.
Friends, with him I see the world for the first time.
My little swallow sits there. Above, the shining,
Warming sun; below, the blooming, breathing earth.
The flowers, the trees, the roofs,
Distant forests, telegraph wires,
All, all their silent heads
Bowed in greeting.

The ripening ears corn rustle
Even I the prisoner.
The blue sky of summer curves too
Over this dead yard.
I breathe
In the sweet joy of noon.

Earth! Beloved.

Vom mutigen Jungen lernen die Geschwister.
Wie es mit schöner Geduld ihnen hilft!

Und noch ein paar Tage später tummeln sich
Draußen Alte und Junge.

In heiteren Spielen lernen die Jungen des Fluges
Festliche Kunst ...

Abends kehrten sie nicht mehr heim.

The siblings learn from their brave brother
That it helps to have patience!

And a few days later the old and young
Still romp about outside.

In buoyant games the young learn flight's
Festive art . . .

They don't come home in the evening.

Lausche ich Euch, Schwalben,
Lächle ich meines werkenden Tuns.

Der Mensch Mitte des Weltalls?
Warum nicht die Schwalbe!
Erhebet doch, erhebet doch
Die Schwalbe
Auf den Thron des siebenten Tages.

Um des Menschen willen
Habt Ihr Menschen gemordet,
Um der Schwalbe willen,
Vielleicht, daß Ihr den Menschen findet.
Und mehr als den Menschen.

Lausche ich Euch, Schwalben,
Lächle ich meines werkenden Tuns.
Lächle auch Du, Freund.

I listen to you, swallows,
I smile as I go about my tasks.

The man in the middle of the world?
Why not the swallow!
Rise, raise
The swallow
On the throne of the seventh day.

Murdered man
For the sake of men,
For the sake of the swallow
That you may find man.
Perhaps more than men.

I listen to you, my swallows,
Smiling as I go about my tasks.
You smile back, friend.

Und wieder richten die Schwalben das Nest.

Und wieder Tage werbender Liebe, trunkener Erfüllung.

Und wieder ward mir friedliche Beglückung.

Aber draußen kämpfen die Brüder ...

And again the swallows prepare their nest.

And again days of love, drunken passion.

And again I'm full of joy.

But outside, our brothers fighting . . .

Vier Junge, blind noch, zittern im Nest.
Immer seltener kehren die Eltern heim.
Not! Not!
Keine Nahrung für die Jungen in der Erloschenheit
Nebliger Tage.
Not! Not!
Am Abend schmiegen sich nackte Leiberchen
An die mütterliche Brust, so hilflos vertrauend,
Als schmiegten sich Sterbende ans Herz
Inbrünstig geträumter Gottheit.
Die Schwälbin weinte.

Mensch, sahest Du je ein Tier weinen?

Four hatchlings, still blind, shiver in the nest.
The parents hardly come home.
Woe! Woe!
No food for those in the fog
Of extinction.
Woe! Woe!
In the evening, they nestle their little bodies
Against their mother's breast, helpless, as though
The dying huddled against the heart
Of a dreamed-up god.
The swallow weeps.

God, have you ever seen an animal cry?

Frost kam über Nacht
In einem Leichenmantel.

Am Morgen bin ich aufgewacht.
Das Nest war leer ...
Mein Herz war leer ...

O liebe kleine Schwälbchen

Frost came overnight
In a burial shroud.

In the morning I awake.
The nest was empty . . .
My heart was empty . . .

Oh my lovely little swallows

Die Schwalbeneltern trauern um ihre Jungen.
In einer sehr wehen Nähe kauern sie auf dem Draht, der sich über meinen Tisch spannt.
Eines schenkt dem andern die Wärme seines Blutes.
Anders trauert Ihr, meine Schwalben, als Menschen trauern.
Eure Klage: ein frierendes Erschauern vor dem Hauche der Unendlichkeit.
Mit Euch trauert der dämmernde Abend.
Mit Euch trauern die Dinge meiner Zelle.

Erhabenes Schweigen

The parents mourn their young.
Huddled close on the wire that stretches
above my table.
One gives the other the warmth of his blood.
You mourn differently, my swallows, than people.
Your lament: a cold shudder in the breath of
Infinity.
The twilight mourns with you.
The things of my cell mourn with you.

Sublime silence sinking

Nicht trage
In Nächten der Verfinsterung
Sehnsucht
Nach Menschen.
Fürchte das Wort, das erwürgt!

Wahrlich,
Erst wen Du nennst,
Stirbt Deiner Seele ganz.

Do not carry
A longing
For people
Into desire's eclipse.
Fear the word that strangles.

Truly,
Only when you name it,
Does your soul trickle out.

Schon wehen herbstliche Stürme
Über die schwäbischen Felder,
Taumeln in Lüften
Heimatlose Blätter.
Aus sumpfigen Moosen der Donau
Steigen die Nebel,
Brauend
Den fahlen Mantel
Unendlicher Totenklage.

Zum Winterflug
Sammeln sich die Schwalben.

Zur Winterstille
Sammelt sich mein Herz.

Autumnal storms already
Streaming across Swabian fields,
Homeless leaves
Tumble through the air.
Fog rises
From the swampy mosses of the Danube,
Brewing
The pale cloak of
Endless mourning.

The swallows gather
For their winter flight.

My heart gathers
For the silence of winter.

Ein letztes Mal noch höre ich der Schwalben Lied:

Unter Myriaden Häusern werden wir im Frühling
dieses graue Hafthaus finden
Unter Myriaden Zellen werden wir im Frühling
deine Zelle finden

One last time I hear the swallows' song.

Among myriad houses we will find
  this gray prison in the spring
Among myriad cells we will find
  your cell in the spring

Nun habt Ihr mich verlassen, liebste Gefährten Ihr meiner Haft.
Wie war die Zelle warm von Eurer flirrenden Melodie, vom Atem Eurer Körperchen, von den tönenden Ellipsen Eures stürzenden Fluges.
Ihr kosmischen Gefährten meines Sommers,
Geliebteste Ihr,
Fernste,
Nächste,
In demütiger Dankbarkeit
Denke ich Eurer schenkenden Liebe.

Tierchen nennen die Menschen Euch,
Und es schwingt ein Überhebliches in ihrer Stimme, wenn sie Tierchen sagen.
O über ihre Torheit!
Ich habe gelernt andächtig zu werden vor Eurem unnennbaren Tiersein.

Bevor nicht die Menschen wiederfinden den Grund ihrer Tierheit,
Bevor sie nicht sind
Sind
Wird ihr Kampf nur wert sein
Neuen Kampfes,
Und noch ihre heiligste Wandlung
Wird wert sein neuer Wandlung.

Now you've left me, you dearest comrades.
How was this cell so warm from your flickering melody,
from the breath of your little bodies, from the sonorous ellipses of your tumbling flight.
You cosmic companions of my summer,
Your beloved,
Far,
Near,
In humble thanks
I think of the gift of your love.

People call you animals,
And there's something smug in their voices when they say it.
What fools!
I have learned to revere your unspeakable animality.

Before people find the reason for their animal nature,
Before they are not and
Are.
Their struggle will only count if it births
A new struggle,
And even their most sacred transformation
Will birth only further change.

VORMORGEN

Der Ringende

TOWARD MORNING

VERSE VOM FRIEDHOF

An die Freunde

Was ist ein Jahr, und was ist eine Stunde
Im Acker Zeit, der brach zu unsern Füßen liegt.

GRAVEYARD VERSE

Dearest friends,
What is a year, and what is an hour,
in the time of the field that lies fallow under our feet.

DER RINGENDE

Mutter, Mutter,
Warum bist Dus nicht?

Kann ich nicht jene Frau,
Die mir mit ihrem Blute
In dunklen Nächten Herzschlag lieh,
Aus frommem Herzen Mutter nennen,
So will ich weite Wege wandern.
O, daß ich einst vom Suchen nicht ermüdet,
An stachlichen Ligusterhecken träumend,
Dich, Mutter, fände.

Bin ich nicht selbst mir Mutter?
Du, Frau, gabst stöhnend
Einmal Leben mir,
Ich starb so oft seit jenem Tag,
Ich starb
Gebar mich
Starb
Gebar mich

Ich ward mir Mutter.

MARSCHLIED

Wir Wandrer zum Tode,
Der Erdnot geweiht,
Wir kranzlose Opfer
Zu Letztem bereit,

Wir Preis einer Mutter,
Die nie sich erfüllt,
Wir wunschlose Kinder
Von Schmerzen gestillt,

Wir Tränen der Frauen,
Wir lichtlose Nacht,
Wir Waisen der Erde
Ziehn stumm in die Schlacht.

END OF THE STRUGGLE

Mother mother,
Why's it not you?

Each woman who lends me
her heartbeat
on dark nights,
can I not call her mother?
So will I walk long, long roads.
Oh, that I didn't tire of searching,
Dreaming of thorny hedges,
Where, Mother, I would find you.

Am I not myself my mother?
You, woman, groan
Once and gave me life.
I've died so often since that day,
I die
Birth me
Died
Birthed me

I became my mother

MARCHING SONG

We wanderers of death,
Doomed to the earth,
Our crownless offering
Ready to the last,

We're the praise of a mother,
That never comes true,
We wishless children
Of sorrow's breast,

We tears of women,
We lightless night,
We orphans of earth
Slide silent into war.

MORGEN

Feldküchen.
Fahrer schlafhockend
Knarren in Morgen hinein,
Der schwer
Die nachtverschlungnen Glieder löst.
In seinem Strahlenhauch
Wiegt sich der Buchen Gezweig.
Lichtgetaucht
Atmet der Himmel ...
Blaudunst verhüllt den Mont-Sec.
Nebelfetzen
Trauerfahnen
Über Schützengräben.
Menschenleiber
Verstümmelte Menschenleiber...
Sonne steigt empor.

GESCHÜTZWACHE

Sternenhimmel.
Gebändigtes Untier
Glänzt mein Geschütz,
Glotzt mit schwarzem Rohr
Zum milchigen Mond.
Käuzchen schreit.
Wimmert im Dorf ein Kind.
Geschoß,
Tückischer Wolf,
Bricht ins schlafende Haus.
Lindenblüten duftet die Nacht.

MORNING

Field-kitchens.
Drivers curled asleep,
creaking into morning.
The weight
of night-twisted limbs undone.
In its glowing breath
the beech branches sway.
Lightdrenched
Breathes the sky —
A blue haze clouds Montsec.
The fog is shreded.
By flags of mourning
Human bodies
Strewn over trenches.
Mutilated corpses —
Sun rises up.

GUARD DUTY

Starry sky.
My gun a
Tamed beast,
Glistening barrel
To the milky moon.
Owls shriek.
A child whines in the village.
Bullet,
Treacherous wolf,
Breaks through a sleeping house.
The night smells of bleeding lindens.

GANG ZUM SCHÜTZENGRABEN

Durch Granattrichter,
Schmutzige Pfützen,
Stapfen sie.
Über Soldaten,
Frierend im Erdloch,
Stolpern sie.

Ratten huschen pfeifend übern Weg,
Sturmregen klopft mit Totenfingern
An faulende Türen.
Leuchtraketen
Pestlaternen ...
Zum Graben zum Graben.

GANG ZUR RUHESTELLUNG

Mann hinter Mann
Torkelt im Laufgraben.
Gepäck drückt müde Knochen.
An Kleidern frißt Lehm.
In grauen Gesichtern stumpfen Augen.
Irgendwer stolpert, fällt hin.
Am Waldfriedhof Sammeln.
Einer träumt am Massengrab
»Solchen Haufen Weihnachtskuchen
Wünscht ich mir als Kind,
Soviel« ...
Vierzehn Kumpel zerbrach eine Mine.
Wann wars doch?
Gestern.

STELLUNGSKRIEG

Alltag hämmert,
Würgt Dich,
Daß Müdsein ins Blut dringt.
Lichter dunsten fahl.
Trotz krepiert.
Letzten Kampf ersehnst Du.

WALK TO THE TRENCHES

Through grenade craters,
and muddy puddles
They trudge.
Over soldiers
Freezing in foxholes,
They stumble.

Rats whistle like arrows across the path,
Stormrain knocks with dead fingers
On rotting doors.
The signal flares of
Plague lanterns...
From ditch to ditch.

TOWARD REST

Man after man
Staggering through trenches.
Baggage pinching white knuckles.
Mud eats at our clothes.
Dull eyes in gray faces.
Somebody stumbles, falls.
Is collected by the dead.
Somebody dreams of mass graves
"As a child I'd wished for
Such a pile of Christmas cakes,
So many. . ."
Fourteen comrades set off a mine.
When was that again?
Yesterday.

TRENCH WARFARE

The everyday pounds in your ears,
Choking you, so
Exhaustion enters your blood.
The light a pale mist.
Still you crave the last fight
In spite of death.

KONZERT

Marmorpfeiler gischten zu kristallnen Säulen,
Decke wölbt sich zum bestirnten Firmament,
Vom Sturz der Töne überflutet
Versinkt Parkett, Getäfel flackernd brennt,
Menschen kleben nackt auf Strohgeflechten,
Gesichter fließen, leuchten fernem Traum,
In fruchtbeschwerten Augen kreist Gebären,
Geschicke brodeln hüllenlos im Raum …

LEICHEN IM PRIESTERWALD

Ein Düngerhaufen faulender Menschenleiber:
Verglaste Augen, blutgeronnen,
Zerspellte Hirne, ausgespiene Eingeweide,
Die Luft verpestet vom Kadaverstank,
Ein einzig grauenvoller Wahnsinnschrei!

O Frauen Frankreichs,
Frauen Deutschlands,
Säht Ihr Eure Männer!
Sie tasten mit zerfetzten Händen
Nach den verquollnen Leibern ihrer Feinde,
Gebärde, leichenstarr, ward brüderlicher Hauch,
Ja, sie umarmen sich.
O schauerlich Umarmen!

Ich sehe, sehe, bleibe stumm.
Bin ich ein Tier, ein Metzgerhund?
Geschändete …
Gemordete …

ALP

Auf einer Stange morsch und faul
Hockt das Völkergewissen,
Um die Stange tanzen drei Kinderknochen,
Aus dem Leib einer jungen Mutter gebrochen,
Es blökt den Takt das Schaf bäh bäh.

CONCERT

Marble columns pour up, splay into
Crystal ceiling, curving to the stellar firmament.
The plunge of notes overflows, floods
The parquetry, the wainscotting burns, flickering.
People are glued naked to straw.
Faces melting, light like a distant dream.
Birth circles round fruit-laden eyes.
Fate seeths, homeless in space.

BODIES IN THE BOIS-LE-PRÊTRE

A dung-heap of rotting human bodies.
Glazed eyes, blood clots,
Split brains, spewed entrails,
The stench of corpses pollutes the air,
A single gruesome shriek.

O women of France,
Women of Germany,
Look at your men!
With shredded hands they grope
For the swollen corpses of the enemy,
Their gesture, like rigor mortis, was a common breath.
Yes, they embraced each other.
Gruesome embrace.

I see, see, sink silent.
Am I an animal? A butcher's dog?
Dishonored . . .
Murdered . . .

NIGHTMARE

Rotten and decayed, the people's conscience
Perches atop a pole. The bones of children
Dance around the pole.
Broken from the flesh of a young mother,
It bleats to the beat of a sheep: bah bah.

MENSCHEN

Krieg verjährte zum Gespenst,
Das knöchern seine Finger
Um die gekreisten Völker krallte.
Menschen taten von sich ihre Hüllen,
Leeren Auges starrten sie gekuppelt,
Keiner war, der Bruder lächeln mochte,
Keiner, der dem andern seine Arme bot,
Worte, die sie sprachen, waren Masken,
So saßen sie beisammen,
Mumien oder Grammophone.

AN DIE DICHTER

Anklag ich Euch, Ihr Dichter,
Verbuhlt in Worte, Worte, Worte!
Ihr wissend nickt mit Greisenköpfen,
Berechnet Wirbelwirkung, lächelnd und erhaben,
Ihr im Papierkorb feig versteckt!
Auf die Tribüne, Angeklagte!
Entsühnt Euch!
Sprecht Euch Urteil!
Menschkünder Ihr!
Und seid ...?
So sprecht doch! Sprecht!

DEN MÜTTERN

Mütter,
Eure Hoffnung, Eure frohe Bürde
Liegt in aufgewühlter Erde,
Röchelt zwischen Drahtverhauen,
Irret blind durch gelbes Korn.
Die auf Feldern jubelnd stürmten,
Torkeln eingekerkert, wahnsinnschwärend,
Blinde Tiere durch die Welt.
Mütter!
Eure Söhne taten das einander.

PEOPLE

War became a specter
That cracks its fingers
Round the people.
They shed their skin,
Staring empty eyed, interlinked.
Nobody smiled,
No body extended an arm to another.
The words they spoke were masks.
But they sat together.
Mummies or gramophones.

TO THE POETS

I denounce you, poets,
Wrapped up in words, words, words.
You nod along with your aged heads,
Eyeing the vortex, smiling, sublime
Cowards buried in the trash.
The defendant may now take the stand.
Repent!
Speak your verdict!
You *prophets!*
Well, are you . . .?
Speak. Speak!

THE MOTHERS

Mothers,
Your hope, your joyous burden
Lies in the churning earth,
The death rattle of barbed wire
Wandering blind through yellowed wheat.
They who happily stormed the fields
Lurch, incarcerated, festering madness.
Blind animals through the world.
Mothers,
Your sons did this to each other.

Grabt Euch tiefer in den Schmerz,
Laßt ihn zerren, ätzen, wühlen,
Recket gramverkrampfte Arme,
Seid Vulkane, glutend Meer:
Schmerz gebäre Tat!

Euer Leid, Millionen Mütter,
Dien als Saat durchpflügter Erde,
Lasse keimen
Menschlichkeit.

ICH HABE EUCH UMARMT

Ich habe Euch umarmt mit Flammenhänden,
Worte wurden blutdurchpulste Speere,
Die Euch
Zum Lichte, rauschendem, erlösten.
Ihr Tausende, fabrikgemartert, Arbeitssielen,
Ihr wurdet einzig strahlend Auge,
Ihr wurdet einzige gestraffte Hand,
Die ich ergriff in brünstiger Umklammrung –
Ich spreche Ich?
Sprach ich zu Euch?
Der Mensch,
Der farbige Ellipsen um Sonnenbälle fliegt,
Er sprach zu Euch.
Der Mensch!
Der Mensch!

ÜBER MEINER ZELLE

Über meiner Zelle
Stapfen schwere
Nägelbeschlagne Schritte
Hin und her.
Immer ...
Ruhelos ...

Bruder, möchte ich rufen.
Wird er mich hören?
Ein kleines Mädchen
Bog ängstlich sich fort
Und versteckte sein Köpfchen.

Dig deeper into this pain.
Let it etch into you, tear at you, dig into your
Grief-stricken arms.
Be volcanoes, blazing seas.
Pain births action.

Your suffering, millions of mothers
Serves as the crop of the sown earth.
Let humanity
Sprout.

I'VE EMBRACED YOU

I've embraced you with flaming hands.
Words were the pulsing blood of spears
Which rushed you
Back to the light.
You thousands, factory martyrs, labor casualties.
You were once a luminous eye,
Once a tightened hand
I grasped in the heat of embrace —
I spoke? I
Spoke to you?
The man
Who reels iridescent ellipses around the sun.
He spoke to you.
The man.
That man.

ABOVE MY CELL

Above my cell
Heavy,
Steel-toed steps
Stomp to and fro.
Always . . .
Restless . . .

Brother, were I to call
Would you hear me?
A little girl
Anxiously turns away
And hides her little head.

DEUTSCHLAND

Durch das Gitter meiner Zelle
Seh ich Kinder spielen.
Eingespannt in enge Zelle,
Kerkerjahre … Marterjahre …

Deutschland,
Deine Söhne werden
Viele Jahre
Nicht mit Kindern spielen.

ZWEI TAFELN

Den Toten der Revolution

Todgeweihte Leiber
trotzig gestemmt
Wider den Bund
der rohen Bedränger,
Löschte Euch Schicksal
mit dunkler Geberde.
Wer die Pfade bereitet,
stirbt an der Schwelle,
Doch es neigt sich vor ihm
in Ehrfurcht der Tod.

Den Lebenden

Euch ziemt nicht
Trauern,
Euch ziemt nicht
Verweilen,
Euch ward Vermächtnis,
Getränkt
Vom Herzblut der Brüder,
Euer
Wartet die schaffende
Tat.
Lastend
Bedränget den Nacken
Die Zeit.
Aufsprengt
Dem helleren Morgen
Die Tore!

GERMANY

Through the bars of my cell
I can see children playing.
Trapped in a narrow cell,
Caged years . . . Martyred years . . .

Germany,
Your sons will
Not play with children
For many years.

FOUR TABLEAUX

The Dead of the Revolution

Bodies doomed to
death pressed against
raw oppression,
Fate erased your fate
with a single glance.
Who pioneers the path,
dies on the threshold.
Though it it slants before him
in reverence of death.

The Living

It's not fit
To mourn,
It's not fit
To dwell,
You were soaked
In the blood
Of your brothers,
You
Await the
Procreant signal.
Heavy
Hangs the neck
Of time.
Open
The bright gates
Of morning!

REQUIEM DEN GEMORDETEN BRÜDERN

GROSSER CHOR:

Senkt die roten Fahnen!
Fahnen der Freiheit!
Fahnen der Liebe!
Fahnen des Anbruchs!
Senkt sie zur Erde,
Dem blutigen Schoße
Der allumfassenden Mutter!

EINE WEIBLICHE STIMME:

Eingezwängt ins Joch der Unterdrückten,
Jahre tief umspült von Not,
Kerker der Fabriken sie umdroht,
Matten ihre Augen, die verzückten.

Nächte dumpfen in verschwitzten Stuben,
Frauen gehen schwanger wie ein welker Wind,
Welt wird taub und stumm und blind,
Siecher Tod in falben Gruben.

EINE KINDERSTIMME:

Traurig war von Wünschen unerfüllten,
Frühling uns und ohne Sonnenstern,
Märchenbuch und Spielzeug lag im Laden fern,
Keine Mütter, die den Hunger stillten.

EINE MÄNNLICHE STIMME:

Morgen kommt! Da springen auf die Zellen!
Volk der Arbeit dröhnet schweren Schritt,
Tausendfach geballter Tod geht mit,
Um den goldnen Baum zu fällen.

Eine weibliche Stimme:

Tag wird! hell umloht von leuchtender Geberde,
Lied der Freiheit tönet ans verzückte Ohr,
Mutter preist den Sohn, den sie verlor,
Daß er Dünger werd dem Acker neuer Erde.

GROSSER CHOR:

Wir grüßen die rosigen Hügel
Befreiten Tags!
Die Ketten zersprengt!
Die Ketten zersprengt!

REQUIEM TO OUR FALLEN BROTHERS

CHORUS:

Lower the red flags!
Flags of freedom!
Of love!
Flags of dawn!
Sink to the earth,
To the blood-red womb
Of our all-encompassing mother.

A WOMAN'S VOICE:

Years steeped in woe
Wedged deep in the yoke of the oppressed,
Threatened by the prisons of factories,
Their eyes gone dull, entrapped.

Nights drenched in forgotten rooms,
Pregnant women walk like ripped fog,
The world is deaf and dumb and blind,
Certain death in fallow graves.

A CHILD'S VOICE::

We were sad. Wishes unfulfilled.
Spring and no sun.
Fairy tales and toys locked in the shop.
No mother to still our hunger.

A MAN'S VOICE:

Morning comes! Pounce on the cells!
The workers drum their heavy steps,
A thousandfold, clenched death follows
To fall a golden tree.

A WOMAN'S VOICE:

Daylight comes! Wrapped in a bright gesture,
The song of freedom resounds on rapt ears.
A mother mourns the son she's lost,
That he may be manure for an acre of new earth.

CHORUS:

We greet the auroral hills of
Liberated day!
Break your chains and
The chains break!

Brüder geleitet die Schwestern!
Beginnet das Werk!
Wir grüßen die rosigen Hügel
Befreiten Tags!

Eine männliche Stimme:
Stellet Wachen aus!
Noch ist der Sieg nicht unser,
Feind gepanzert wälzt sich gegen uns,
Giftges Gas schickt er in gelben Schwaden,
Flammen speit sein Eisenmund.

Eine weibliche Stimme:
Wehe, sie gürten sich!
Wehe, Dämmerung hüllt sie!
Wehe und Fluch dem Krieg!
Wehe dem Haß!
Mensch gegen Mensch,
Bruder mordet den Bruder,
Wehe, die zarte Blüte,
Eben geboren, erfriert.

Chor der Männer:
Sie zwingen Kampf uns auf,
Nicht Jubel grüßt den Krieg,
Die Waffe blinder Unvernunft.
Ihr Räte seid bereit
Der Arbeit Werk zu schützen.

Einige Frauen:
Wir sind so tief dem Grauenvollen abgewendet,
Der Mund verstummt, kein Siegeslied geleitet Euch.
Zerbrecht die Eisenwaffen, Männer!
Zerbrecht die Waffen der verwesten Zeit!

Wehe, sie hören nicht!
Dämmerung hüllt sie!
Wehe, das Morden beginnt!

Eine weibliche Stimme:
Verhüllet das Antlitz, Schwestern,
Ich singe ein traurig Lied.
Ich höre Eurer Männer dumpfe Schritte,
Wie Sklaven tragen sie die Hände überm Haupt,

Brothers lead their sisters!
Onto your work!
We greet the rose-red hills of
Liberated day.

A Man's Voice:
To your posts!
Victory is not yet ours
An armored enemy rolls against us
It sends yellow plumes of poison gas,
Spewing fire from it's iron mouth.

A Woman's Voice:
Alack! They approach
Girdled by dusk!
Fuck the war.
Fuck this hatred.
Man against man,
Brother murders brother,
Alas, gentle flower,
Just born, frostbitten.

Chorus of Men:
They bring the battle to us,
No joy to greet it.
Weapons of blind unreason.
Our councils are prepared
To protect our work.

Some Women:
The horrors, our aversion is Orphic,
Mouth sealed shut, no song to guide you to victory.
Men, break the iron weapons!
Break the weapons of decaying time!

Alas, they can't hear!
The dusk envelopes them.
Woe! The killings begin!

A Woman's Voice:
Veil your faces, sisters,
I sing a song of sorrow.
I hear the muffled steps of your men
Like slaves, hands behind their heard

Wie Sklaven werden vorwärts sie gestoßen,
O Schwestern,
Nacht erwürgte Licht.

CHOR DER MÄNNER:
aus der Ferne
An Mauern sterben wir,
In Kerkern erschlagen von Kolben,
Aufsteht der Moloch,
Drängt sich zwischen Mensch und Mensch ...
O Tod in engen Höfen!
O Tod an Gartenzäunen!
O Tod in schwarzen Kerkern!

EINE MÄNNLICHE STIMME:
aus der Ferne
Hört Ihr des Bruders, des Propheten Stimme?
Von rohen Stößen wund ist sein gequälter Leib,
Sie schlagen ihn, da »Brüder!« er sie nennt,
Gemartert, angenagelt an die Erde!
Hört Ihr des Bruders, des Propheten Stimme,
Ein Stammeln ists, ein wehes Stammeln:
»Erschlagt mich doch! O, daß Ihr Menschen seid!«

CHOR DER MÄNNER:
aus der Ferne
Sie haben ihn getötet.
O Tod in engen Höfen!
O Tod an Gartenzäunen!
O Tod in schwarzen Kerkern!

GROSSER CHOR:
Senkt die roten Fahnen!
Fahnen der Freiheit!
Fahnen der Liebe!
Fahnen des Anbruchs!
Senkt sie zur Erde,
Dem blutigen Schoße
Der allumfassenden Mutter!

EINE WEIBLICHE STIMME:
O niemand, der uns trösten kann,
O niemand, dessen milde Worte
Die große Trauer sanfter bettet.

Like slaves, shoved forward.
O Sisters,
Night strangles light.

Chorus of Men
in the distance:
We die on walls,
Slain by pistons in prisons,
Moloch rises
Stretching from man to man . . .
O, death in narrow fields!
O, death on garden walls!
O, death in black prisons.

A Man's Voice
in the distance:e
Do you hear the voice of your brothers?
His tortured body raw with bruises.
They beat him as he calls them *brothers!*
Martyred, nailed to the earth!
Do you hear the voice of the prophets?
It's a stutter, a labored stutter:
"Beat me! O, that you are men!"

Chorus of Men
in the distance:
They killed him.
O death in narrow fields!
Death on garden walls!
Death in black prisons.

Whole Chorus:
Lower the red flags!
Flags of freedom!
Of love!
Flags of dawn!
Sink to the earth,
To the blood-red womb
Of our all-encompassing mother.

A Woman's Voice:
O nobody to comfort us,
No soft words make a gentle bed
Where this grief could rest.

CHOR DER FRAUEN:

Ihr Schwestern, käme Tod uns zu erlösen!
Wir ewigen Opfer, ewige Verlorne!

CHOR DER JUGEND:

Ihr littet tiefe Trauer,
Ihr vergrämten Frauen,
Doch unsre Stimmen seien Trost,
Fanfaren rufen sie Euch zu:
Verzaget nicht!
Neuer Tag wird Nacht verdrängen,
Pflugschar pflügt die Knechtschaft nieder!
Schmerzensreiche, wunde Frauen,
Denkt in schwesterlicher Trauer
Aller Brüder,
Die Barbarengeist der Zeit
In tausend Tode trieb.

EINE WEIBLICHE STIMME:

Selig sind, die guten Willens starben!

CHOR DER FRAUEN:

Requiescant in pace!

GROSSER CHOR:

Senkt die roten Fahnen!
Fahnen der Freiheit!
Fahnen der Liebe!
Fahnen des Anbruchs!
Senkt sie zur Erde,
Dem blutigen Schoße
Der allumfassenden Mutter.

Chorus of Women:

My sisters, let death deliver us!
We eternal victims, eternally lost!

Chorus of Youth:

You've suffered such sorrow
You mourning women,
Let our voices comfort you
A flourish of trumpets calling out to you:
Don't give up!
A new day will oust the night,
Plows to till your chains!
Sorrowful women,
Mourning all brothers
As sisters
The savage spirit of time
Driving a thousand deaths.

A Woman's Voice:

Blessed are those who died of good will!

Chorus of Women:

Requiescant in pace!

Whole Chorus!:

Lower the red flags
Of freedom
And love!
Flags of dawn!
Sink to the earth,
To the blood-red womb
Of our all-encompassing mother.

LIEDER DER GEFANGENEN

SONGS OF THE IMPRISONED

AN ALLE GEFANGENEN

Dämmerung, Schwester der Gefangenen,
Deine Stille schwingt Melodie.
Auf schmaler Pritsche liege ich und lausche ...
Ich höre Euer Herz klopfen,
Eingekerkert in den Gefängnissen der Kontinente,
Dort ... und dort ... und dort ...
Brüder mir: Kämpfer, Rebellen, – ich grüße Euch.
Eine Welt wollen sie Euch weigern,
Eure Welt aber lebt in Eurem Willen.
Und Euch grüße ich, Brüder in den Kerkern Afrikas und Asiens,
Euch, Brüder, in Zuchthäusern der Erde,
Diebe und Einbrecher, Totschläger und Mörder,
Brüder jetzt eines Schicksals, ich grüße Euch.

Wer kann von sich sagen, er sei nicht gefangen?

Ich höre Euer Herz klopfen
Dort ... und dort ... und dort ...
O wäre mir gegeben zu lauschen
Mit der zeitlosen Liebe des geträumten Gottes,
Ich hörte
Den Einen Herzschlag
Aller menschlichen Geschlechter
Aller Sterne
Aller Tiere
Aller Wälder
Aller Blumen
Aller Steine.

Ich hörte
Den Einen Herzschlag
Alles
Lebendigen.

TO ALL THOSE IMPRISONED

Twilight, sisters of prisoners,
Your silence sings melody.
On a narrow bunk I lie and listen —
I hear your heart knocking,
Imprisoned in the prisons of the continents,
There — and there — and there —
Brothers: fighters, rebels — I welcome you.
Your world they want to refuse you,
Your world is alive in your will.
And I welcome you, brethren in the prisons of Africa and Asia,
You, brothers in the Earth's penitentiaries,
Thieves and burglars, mercenaries and murderers,
Brothers now of one fate, I welcome you.

Who can say that they are not imprisoned?

I hear your heart knocking
There — and there — and there —
Oh if I were to listen
With the timeless love of a dreamt-up god,
I heard
The singular heartbeat
Of all humanity
    Every star
    Every animal
    Every forest
    Every flower
    Every stone.

    I heard
    The singular heartbeat
    Of every
    Living thing.

SCHLAFLOSE NACHT

Metallne Schritte in die Nächte fallen,
Die Posten buckeln durch die Höfe ohne Rast,
Wir lauschen schlaflos in das starre Hallen,
Ein schwarzes Schweigen wächst im schwarzen Glast.
Uns alle wirbelt Zwang durch die Gezeiten,
Uns alle eint der Kreaturen Qual,
O Fluch der Grenzen! Menschen hassen ohne Wahl!
Du Bruder Tod wirst uns vereint geleiten.

DURCHSUCHUNG UND FESSELUNG

Nackten Leib brutalen Blicken preisgegeben,
Betastet uns ein schamlos Greifen feiler Hände,
In Fratzenbündel splittern graue Wände,
Die Pfeilen gleich gen unsre Herzen streben.
Pflockt Arm und Fuß in rostge Kette,
Brennt Narben ein den magren Händen,
Ihr könnt, Ihr könnt den Leib nicht schänden,
Wir stehen frei an der verfemten Stätte!
So standen vor uns die Geweihten,
So starben sie am Rand der Zeiten.

WÄLDER

Ihr Wälder fern an Horizonten schwingend,
Vom abendlichen Hauche eingehüllt,
Wie meine Sehnsucht friedlich euch erfüllt,
Minuten Schmerz der Haft bezwingend.

Ich presse meine Stirn an Eisensäulen,
Die Hände rütteln ihre Unrast wund,
Ich bin viel ärmer als ein armer Hund,
Ich bin des angeschoßnen Tieres Heulen.

Ihr Buchenwälder, Dome der Bedrückten,
Ihr Kiefern, heimatliche, tröstet Leid,
Wie wobet ihr geheimnisvoll um den beglückten
Knaben der fernen Landschaft wundersames Kleid …

SLEEPLESS NIGHT

Metallic footsteps falling in the night,
The guards arched over through the yards without rest.
We eavesdrop sleepless in rigid halls,
A black silence rises from black glass,
We're all tied to the same stake of fate,
We're all spinning darkly through the tides.
We're all united by the torment of creaters!
Oh, fuck set borders! People hate without choice!
You, brother Death, will lead us into unity.

SEARCH AND CAPTURE

Brutal glances exposed the naked body,
A shameless gripping of feeble hands touches us,
Gray walls shiver in a grotesque bundle
To which the arrows of our hearts take aim.
Arms and feet fastened in rusted chains,
Burn scars on skinny hands,
They can, they cannot desecrate the body,
We stand free on the defiled site!
So the devoted stood before us.
So they died on the verge of the promised times.

WOODS

Their forests swinging far on the horizon
Shrouded in the evening's breath
As my desire quietly joins with you,
Minutes to conquer the pain of imprisonment.

I press my forehead against the iron pillars,
Hands shaking their restlessness raw.
I am much poorer than a poor dog.
I am the shot animal's helpless howls.

Your Buchenwalds, domes of the oppressed.
Your pines, melody of the homeland, comforting pain,
How you weaved a wondrous dress in secret
Around the blessed boy in the distant landscape —

SPAZIERGANG DER STRÄFLINGE

Sie schleppen Zellen mit in stumpfen Blicken
Und stolpern wie geblendet im Quadrat,
Gehetzte, die im Steinverlies ersticken,
Gehetzte, die ein Paragraph zertrat.
Im Eck die Wärter träge lauern,
Von Sträuchern rinnt ein trübes Licht,
Das kriecht empor an starren Mauern,
Betastet schlaffe Körper und zerbricht.
Der Himmel öffnet sich wie rote Wunde,
Die brennt und brennt und brennt.

BEGEGNUNG IN DER ZELLE

Dinge, die erst feindlich zu Dir schauen,
Gleich in Späherdienst gezwengte Schergen,
Laden Dich zu Fahrten ein als gute Fergen,
Hegen Dich wie schwesterliche Frauen.

Leise rufen all die kargen Dinge:
Schmale Pritsche und die blauen Wasserkrüge,
Schemel flüstert, daß er gern Dich trüge,
Wintermücken wiegen sich wie Schmetterlinge.

Gitterfenster selbst, das Du verloren
Anstarrtest, während Deine Arme hilflos brachen,
Gitterfenster ruft: Nun, Lieber, schaue,
Wie ich aus Wolken Dir ein Paradies erbaue.

LIED DER EINSAMKEIT

Sie wölbt um meine Seele Kathedralen,
Sie schäumt um mich ein brandend Meer,
Der Gosse sperrt sie sich wie eine Wehr,
Und wie ein Wall beschützt sie meine Qualen.
In ihr fühl ich die Süße abendlicher Stille,
Auf leeren Stunden blüht sie sanftes Feld,
Ihr Schoß gebiert das Wunder der geahnten Welt,
Ein stählern Schwert steilt sich metallner Wille.

WALK OF THE CONVICTS

They lug their cells with dulled looks
And stumble, blind, in the square.
The hunted, smothered by stones,
The prey that trampled a paragraph.
In the corner the watchmen lurk, lazy,
A dull light leaks from the bushes,
Creeps up numb walls,
Touches shattered bodies, and breaks.
The sky opens like a red wound
That burns and burns and burns.

ENCOUNTER IN THE CELL

All the things that first seemed hostile to you
Were spies, minions coerced to
Invite you on rides like good ferrymen
And cherish you like sisterly women.

Softly all the empty things call to you:
Cramped beds come, and blue jugs of water,
Chairs whisper that they'll gladly carry you,
Winter mosquitos weigh the same as butterflies.

Even the grated windows that'd lost you,
Staring, while your arms helplessly broke
A housand bars call out to you: Now love, behold,
How I will build you a paradise from clouds.

SONG OF SOLITUDE

She weaves cathedrals round my soul,
Froths around me like a surging sea,
Catches me in the gutters
And, like a border, contains all suffering.
In her I can feel the sweetness of evening's silence,
On empty hours she'll bloom gentle fields.
She births a wonder to the watching world.
A steel sword plunges its metallic will.

GEFANGENE MÄDCHEN

Wie kleine Dirnen an belebten Straßenecken
Sich schüchtern fast und wieder roh bewegen,
Im Schatten der Laternen sich erst dreister regen
Und den zerfransten Rock kokett verstecken ...

Wie Waisenkinder, die geführt auf Promenaden,
Je zwei und zwei in allzu kurzen grauen
Kleidern verschämt zu Boden schauen
Und Stiche fühlen in den nackten Waden ...

So schlürfen sie umstellt von Wärterinnen,
Die Hüften wiegend auf asphaltnen Kreisen,
Sie streichen heimlich mit Gebärden, leisen,
Das härne Kleid, als strichen sie plissiertes Linnen.

FABRIKSCHORNSTEINE AM VORMORGEN

Sie stemmen ihre Wucht in Dämmerhelle,
Gepanzert recken sie sich steil,
Sie spalten Nebel wie getriebner Keil,
Daß jeder Hauch um sie zerschelle.
Morgen kündet sich mit violettem Lachen,
Himmel füllt ein tiefes Blau,
Sie gleichen Posten, überwachen,
Werden spitz und kahl und grau,
Stehen hilflos da und wie verloren
Im Äther, den ein Gott geboren.

MAUER DER ERSCHOSSENEN

Vor Schrei und Aufschrei krümmte sich die Wand.

Wie aus dem Leib des heiligen Sebastian,
Dem tausend Pfeile tausend Wunden schlugen,
So Wunden brachen aus Gestein und Fugen,
Seit in den Sand ihr Blut verlöschend rann.

Weißes Morden raste durch die Tage,

GIRLS IMPRISONED

Like whores on busy street corners
Almost shy and raw, again they move,
Impudent rain in the shadows of lamplight,
and those frayed skirts coyly hidden —

Like orphans on parade,
Two and two in all too short gray
Dresses, looking to the floor in shame,
Bruises on their bare calves —

So they drink, surrounded by the guardwomen,
Their hips drawing asphalt circles,
With soft gestures they secretly brush
Their hairy dress, as though weaving pleated linen.

SMOKESTACKS AT DAWN

They lift their weight at daybreak,
Armored, they stretch themselves,
Splitting the fog like a wedge
That shatters every breath around them.
Morning arrives with violet laughter,
Sky fills a deep blue,
They resemble sentries, police
Becoming sharp and bleak and gray,
Standing there helpless, lost
In the ether that birthed a god.

WALL OF THE EXECUTED

Buckling under the weight of screams,

Like out of the corpse of St. Sebastian
Thousands of arrows met thousands of wounds,
Wounds erupting from brick and mortar
Since her blood ran fading in the sand.

White murder ripping through the days,

Erde wurde zu bespienem Schoß,
Gott ward arm und nackt und bloß,
Doch die Wand in starrer Klage,
Mutter allem Menschenschmerz,
Nahm die Opfer leise an ihr stummes Herz.

GEFANGENER UND TOD

GEFANGENER SPRICHT:

Ich denke Dich, o Tod:
Um mich bricht der Zellenbau in Trümmer,
Aus Pfosten reißen sich
Die Eisengitter los
Und krümmen sich
Im starren Licht.
O, daß ich fliehen könnte!
Denn Dir hilflos hingegeben,
Heißt hilflos sich zerstören,
Wer sich aufgibt,
Wählt Dich zum Freund,
Ich aber will das Leben!

TOD SPRICHT:

Da Du das Leben willst, warum Erbleichen,
Wenn meine Melodie in deiner Seele tönt?
Wer mich erträgt, der atmet wie versöhnt,
Der wird den Sternen seine Hände reichen.

Ist tot der Baum im Herbst der Abendweiten?
Ist tot die Blume, deren Blüte fallend sich erfüllt?
Ist tot der schwarze Stein, der Flammenkräfte hüllt?
Ist tot die Erde über Gräbern menschlicher Gezeiten?

O, sie belogen Dich! Auch ich bin Leben,
So sprachen sie: der Tod sei aus der Welt.
Ich bin der Sinn der Formen, die Vollendung weben,
Dem Einen nahe, das im Schweigen quellt.

The earth became a sacred womb,
God was blind and poor and naked,
And the wall in stark contrast:
The mother of suffering
Lifting all casualties to her silent heart.

PRISONER AND DEATH

The Prisoner speaks.

I think of you, O Death, and
The cell block crumbles around me.
Iron rails rip themselves
Loose from their jambs
And warp
In the numb light.
Oh, that I could flee!
Helplessly giving up
Means helpless self destruction.
Who gives up
Chooses you as a friend.
But I want life!

Death speaks.

You who want life, why do you pale
If my melody rings through your soul?
Who carries me breathes reconciliation,
His hands will reach the stars.

Is the tree dead in autumn at this angle of the sun?
Is the flower dead once petals fall in bloom?
Is the black stone dead that holds the power of fire?
Is the earth dead above graves of humanity?

Oh, they've lied to you! I too am life,
It has been said: Death will be in the world.
I am the meaning of forms that weaves perfection,
Approaching the one who is soaked in silence.

PFADE ZUR WELT

Wir leben fremd den lauten Dingen,
Die um die Menge fiebernd kreisen,
Wir wandern in den stilleren Geleisen
Und lauschen dem Verborgnen, dem Geringen,

Wir sind dem letzten Regentropfen hingegeben,
Den Farbentupfen rundgeschliffner Kieselsteine,
Ein guter Blick des Wächters auslöscht das Gemeine,
Wir fühlen noch im rohen Worte brüderliches Leben.

Ein Grashalm offenbart des Kosmos reiche Fülle,
Die welke Blume rührt uns wie ein krankes Kind,
Der bunte Kot der Vögel ist nur eine Hülle

Des namenlosen Alls, dem wir verwoben sind.
Nachtwind weht menschlich Lachen aus der Ferne,
Und uns berauscht die hymnische Musik der Sterne.

SCHWANGERES MÄDCHEN

Du schreitest wunderbar in mittaglicher Stunde,
Um Deine Brüste rauscht der reife Wind,
Ein Lichtbach über Deinen Nacken rinnt,
Der Sommer blüht auf Deinem Munde.

Du bist ein Wunderkelch der gnadenreichen
Empfängnis liebestrunkner Nacht,
Du bist von Lerchenliedern überdacht,
Und Deine Last ist köstlich ohnegleichen.

SCHWANGERES MÄDCHEN II

Wer wird die Hand Dir halten am verheißnen Tag,
Da sich Dein Leib aufbäumt in roten Bränden?
Ich seh Dein Auge, das vom rohen Wort erschrak,
Ich seh die Nächte irren auf den tauben Wänden,
Ich seh die Wärterin, die ohne Scham
Das heimatlose Kind von Deinen Brüsten nahm.

PATHS TO THE WORLD

We live outside the loud things
That circle feverish around the crowd,
We follow the quieter tracks
And listen in shadows to the little things.

We surrendered to the last raindrops,
To the darkened spots on smoothened pebbles,
A solid glance from the guard empties the commons,
We still feel fraternal life in raw words.

A blade of grass reveals the riches of the kosmos,
A wilting flower pulls on us like a sick child,
The colorful shit of the birds is only a shell

Of the nameless universe into which we're woven.
Nightwind blowing human laughter from the distance,
And we are drunk on the hymnal music of the stars.

PREGNANT GIRL

You stride wondrous through the afternoon,
The ripening wind rushes round your breasts,
A stream of light runs over your neck,
Summer blooming in your mouth.

You are a chalice of the
Conception of the lovedrunk night,
You are drenched in lark song
And your demands delicious beyond compare.

PREGNANT GIRL II

Who will hold your hand on the promised day
As your body arches into crimson flames?
I see your eye, shocked by the unwrought word,
I see nights running blind over deaf walls.
I see the warden who, without shame
Took the orphaned child from your breast.

DÄMMERUNG

Am frühen Abend lischt das Leuchten Deiner Zelle,
Von grauen Wänden gleiten schlanke Schatten,
Wer trotzig schrie, wird träumerisch ermatten,
Die braune Stille schwingt wie eine milde Welle.

Und oft erfüllt den engen Raum opalne Helle,
Gestalten locken Dich zu heitrem Reigen,
Da wird ein Tanz im schweren Mantel Schweigen,
Da wird ein Klang im dämmernden Gefälle.

NÄCHTE

Nächte bergen stilles Weinen,
Pocht wie Kindertritt an Deine Wand,
Lauschst erschreckt: Will jemand Deine Hand?
Weißt: Du reichst sie nur den Steinen.

Nächte bergen Trotz und Stöhnen,
Wilde Sucht nach einer Frau,
Not des Blutes bleicht Dich grau,
Blecken Fratzen, die Dich höhnen.

Nächte bergen niegesungne Lieder,
Nachttau blühn sie, samtne Schmetterlinge,
Küssen die verborgnen Dinge,

Willst sie haschen, sind verweht.

VERWEILEN UM MITTERNACHT

Um Mitternacht erwachst Du. Glocken fallen
Wie Stürme an die Schwelle Deines Traums,
Unendlich schwingt das Leben im Gefäß des Raums,
Ob allen Sternen muß Dein Herzschlag hallen.

Es steigen an die Klänge, die sich ründen,
Die alte Stadt fühlt hilflos die gewordne Zeit,
Sie beugt sich tief: sie ist bereit
Im Schoß der Quelle einzumünden.
Hinschwingt ein letzter Klang in ferne Sphären ...

TWILIGHT

In early evening the light of your cell expires,
Slender shadows slide from gray walls.
Should you scream, you'll tire dreamily.
The brown silence sinks like a soft wave.

And often an opal brightness fills the narrow space
Shapes of your heart call you to dance:
There shall be a dance in the heavy mantle of silence,
There shall be a sound for the fall of twilight.

NIGHTS

Nights carry stifled crying,
Children's footsteps pound on your wall,
Listening, awestruck: does someone want your hand?
Know: you can only give it to the stones.

Nights carry defiance and moans
Wild desire for a woman,
Beating heart bleaches you gray.
Teeth bared, scolding you.

The nights carry unsung songs,
Velvet butterflies bloom on the dew,
Kissing the buried things.

Try to catch them, they blow away.

TO LINGER AT MIDNIGHT

You wake at midnight. Bells falling
Like thunder on the threshold of your dream.
Endlessly life flickers in the container of the room,
As if all the stars echo his heartbeat.

It rises to the sounds taking shape.
Helplessly the old town feels the turning time,
She bows deeply, she is ready
To enter the womb of the spring.
A final sound swinging into distant spheres.

Der Wandernde verweilt und lauscht:
Nur tiefe Stille wird gebären,
Wer in der Erde wurzelt, rauscht.

NOVEMBER

Städte sind sehr fern, darin die Menschen leben.
Knäuel würgt die Kehle Dir, Grauen
Betastet Deine Glieder. Wer wird Freiheit schauen?
Wann endlich wird sich dieses Sklavenvolk erheben?

GEFANGENER REICHT DEM TOD DIE HAND

Erst spitzer Schrei der armen Kreatur,
Dann poltern Flüche durch die Gänge,
Sirenen singen die Alarmgesänge,
In allen Zellen tickt die Totenuhr.

Was trieb Dich, Freund, dem Hein die Hand zu reichen?
Wimmern der Geschlagnen? Die geschluchzten Hungerklagen?
Jahre, die wie Leichenratten unsern Leib zernagen?
Ruhelose Schritte, die zu unsern Häuptern schleichen?

Trieb Dich der stumme Hohn der leidverfilzten Wände,
Der wie ein Nachtmahr unsre Brust bedrückt?
Wir wissens nicht. Wir wissen nur, daß Menschenhände

Einander wehe tun. Daß keine Hilfe überbrückt
Die Ströme Ich und Du. Daß wir den Weg verlieren
Im Dunkel dieses Hauses. Daß wir frieren.

NACHT

Zinnoberroter Traum emporreißt unterdrückte Lust,
Die wandgeketteten verdammten Pritschen stöhnen,
O, nun auftauchen Bilder, die den kahlen Raum verschönen,
Der Dämon wühlt in unsrer Brust.

Erwachend höhnen, Kupplerinnen, uns die Eisengitter,
Im Morgengrauen sind die Zellen wie verweinte Mütter.

The wanderer lingers and listens:
Only a deep silence will be born
Which rustles, rooted in the earth.

NOVEMBER

Cities where people live are far.
A ball of wool to choke you gray, a horror
Touches your limbs. Who will show them freedom?
When will this slave people finally rise up?

PRISONER REACHES A HAND TOWARD DEATH

First the splitting cry of that poor creature,
Then curses rumble through the halls,
Sirens sing the alarm-song,
The deathwatch ticks in every cell.

What drove you, friend, to reach a hand toward death?
Whimpers of the whipped? The swallowed pangs of hunger?
The years gnawing at our body like rats to a corpse?
Restless footsteps that slink into our heads?

Were you driven by the mute mockery of grief-ridden walls,
That push on our chest like a nightmare?
We do not know. We only know that human hands

Harm one another. That no bridge straddles
The rivers I and You. That we lose the way
In the dark of this house. That we are cold.

NIGHT

Cinnibar red dreams tear up suppressed appetite
The damn walled-in bunks moan,
O, now pictures emerge to decorate the naked room
A demon nuzzling into our chest

Iron bars to mock you when you wake, matchmakers,
The cells are like crying mothers at dawn.

GEMEINSAME HAFT

Gepfercht in einen schmalen Käfiggang,
Gleich Tieren, die an Gitterstäben wund sich biegen,
Und die vor Heimweh krank am Boden liegen
Und fast erschrecken vor der eignen Stimme Klang,
Dorren sie hin und träge wird ihr Blut,
Nur Giftstrom bricht aus ihrem Munde,
Der sucht und ätzt des Nachbarn Wunde –
Die eingesperrten Menschen sind nicht gut,
Sie werden taub und stumm und blind,
Sie hassen sich, weil sie so einsam sind.

BESUCHER

Augen sind vom Schrei der Mauern
Verstörte Tauben, die ein Marder überfiel,
Und die verschüchtert flattern ohne Ziel.
Herz klammert sich an des Gefangnen Hand,
Immer schlägt es wie verbannt,
Seit Waffenknechte ihn umlauern.
Er aber wuchs aus Last erstarrter Zellen.
Entrückt dem Kreise kleinen Lebens,
Schaut er nach innen, trinkt an Gottes Quellen –

Und der Besucher friert, er kommt vergebens.

ENTLASSENE STRÄFLINGE

Trunkne träumen durch vertraute Gassen,
Gefäß, darin ein Lichtmeer brandet,
In Farben schäumt, im Asphalt strandet –
Form kann die Fülle noch nicht fassen ...
Auferstandne tasten sie mit durstgen Blicken
Nach Knospen, die im Frühlingsatem schwellen ...
Streifen von sich modrig Kleid verwester Zellen,
Wachsen flammend auf in irdischem Entzücken.
Stadt umkrallt sie jäh wie fremde Hand ...
Wieder sind sie tief in sich verklungen ...
Fern die Zeit, da sie gebannt
Im grauen Sarg, dem Wände Totenlied gesungen.
Lächeln still, als ob Erloschenes sie fänden,
Streifen fremdes Kind mit unbeholfnen Händen.

COLLECTIVE CONFINEMENT

Crammed in narrow cages
Like animals bent raw against bars,
And who lie homesick on the floor
Almost afraid of the sound of their voices.
Withering, blood beginning to slow,,
Poison streams from their mouths
Which searches for and etches into a neighbor's open wound —
The prisoners are not well.
They grow deaf and mute and blind,
They hate themselves because they are so alone.

VISITOR

Eyes are pigeons,
frightened by screaming walls.
Those frightened flutter aimlessly,
Heart beating against the prisoner's hand —
Always beating like an exile,
While the soldies stalk around him.
Grown from the weight of fossilized cells,
Removed from this little circle of life
In a reverie, he drinks from the sources of God —

And the visitor is cold, has come in vain.

RELEASED CONVICTS

Dreaming drunk through familiar alleys,
A sea of lights burns inside,
Foaming iridescent against asphalt —
Form cannot grasp this fullness.
The resurrected grope with thirsty sight
For leafbuds swelling in the spring's breath —
Strip themselves of rotting clothes, decaying cells,
Bursting into a fire of wordly delight.
The city grabs you like a stranger's hand —
Again they sink deep into themselves —
Distant is the time when they were paralyzed
In gray coffins, when hollow walls sang the deathsong.
Smiling quietly, as if they found something extinct,
Running their clumsy hands over this new child.

UNSER WEG

Die Klöster sind verdorrt und haben ihren Sinn verloren,
Sirenen der Fabriken überschrillen Vesperklang,
Und der Millionen trotziger Befreiungssang
Verstummt nicht mehr vor klösterlichen Toren.
Wo sind die Mönche, die den Pochenden zur Antwort geben:
»Erlösung ist Askese weltenferner Stille ...« –
Ein Hungerschrei, ein diamantner Wille
Wird an die Tore branden: »Gebt uns Leben!«
Wir foltern nicht die Leiber auf gezähnten Schragen,
Wir haben andern Weg zu Gott gefunden,
Uns sind nicht stammelndes Gebet die Stunden,
Das Reich des Friedens wollen wir zur Erde tragen,
Den Unterdrückten aller Länder Freiheit bringen –
Wir müssen um das Sakrament der Erde ringen!

OUR WAY

The monasteries have decayed and lost their meaning,
The sirens of factories screech over the vespers,
And the millions of defiant liberation songs
No longer fall silent on cloistered gates.
Where are the monks, who answer the throbbing:
"Salvation is the ascetic world-silence..." —
A joint cry of hunger, a single diamond will
Will burn into the gates: Give us Life!
We do not torment the bodies on the scaffold,
We have found another way to the world,
We are not stammering prayers for hours,
We want to bring the kingdom of peace to the earth,
To bring freedom to the oppressed of all countries,
We must struggle for the sacrament of the earth!

UN/
VERÖFFENTLICHTE
GEDICHTE

UN/
PUBLISHED
POEMS

AN DIE SPRACHE

Sprache,
Gefäß göttlichen Geistes.
Weltorgel!
Brausende in allen Registern!
Hauch der Erfüllten,
Stammeln wunder Mütter,
Seziermesser furchtloser Denker,
Dichtergeliebte!
Sie haben Dich geschändet,
In allen Pfützen Europas
Taten Sie Dir Gewalt.
Sie schändeten Dich!
Zeig Dein Gorgonenantlitz den Tempelräubern!
Weh, daß Du Mordschweiß perlst!
Tauch in geheiligten Quell geäderte Glieder
Voll göttlichen Bluts!
Steige verjüngt,
Geheiligt empor!

ABEND AM BODENSEE

In roten Wellenbändern fließen Sonnenstrahlen
Zum perlmuttzarten Horizont, dem letztgeschauten Wall.
Im Norden spielt das Wasser, glänzend wie Metall,
Mit blassen Mondesfingern, die uns Silberteiche malen.
Oft huschen über weite Flächen violette Garben.
Gebirg ruht still, umtönt von weichem Hauch.
Wie schwarze Leichentücher wälzt sich aus Fabriken Rauch –
Ich denke all der Brüder, die zur Abendstunde sterben.
Im Herbst zu sterben ist so schwer, die Bäume glänzen
In brokatner Pracht und lassen glühend tiefre ahnen.
Die Buchenkronen winden sich zu Symphonien von Glutenkränzen,
September-Farbenrausch will uns zu heißem Leben mahnen. –
Ach möchte milde Hand den Brüdern, die im Tode steil sich bäumen,
Erfüllte Ruhe spenden, abendlich verklärtes Träumen.

ON THE LANGUAGE

Language,
Vessel of divine spirit.
Worldorgan!
Thundering in all registers!
Breath of satisfaction,
Wounded mothers babbling,
Scalpels of fearless thinkers,
Beloved poets!!
They have disgraced you,
In all the puddles of Europe
They have violated you.
They desacrated you!
Show your gorgon face to the temple robbers!
Woe, you wear the sheen of deathsweat.
Dip into the sacredspring
The veined limbs of holy blood.
Rise, rejuvenated,
Sanctified!

EVENING ON LAKE CONSTANCE

Sunbeams streaming in red bands of waves
To the pearly-soft horizon, the last wall we saw.
To the north the playful water gleams like metal,
With pale moon-fingers, that paint us silver ponds.
Violet sheaves scurry by across wide fields.
The mountains rest, tinged with a soft breath.
Smoke rolls out of factories like burial shrouds —
I think of all my brothers who've died in the evening hour.
To die in autumn is so difficult, the trees glisten
In brocade splendor, emitting a deep glow.
The crowns of beech trees twist into symphonies of blazing wreathes,
September iridescent, urges us into the fire of life.
Oh to reach a gentle hand to my brothers, to give them peace
Who rise in death, misty-eyed dreams of evening.

MENSCHEN

1.

Als der Krieg sie überfiel wie ein toller Hund,
Schrien sie auf und riefen sich herbei,
Daß sie gemeinsam sich wehrten
Und ihren Willen
Wie einen Flammenfelsen
Dem Kampf entgegen stemmten. –
Oder taten's nur, um sich zu stützen
Und nicht allein zu sein,
So unsagbar allein.

2.

Da prasselten auf ihre Seelen riesengroße Steine.
Sie sahen sich auf uferlosem Meer
Ertrinkende die Arme kläglich recken.
Und fühlten Schmerz an ihrem Herzen zerren.
Den Schuldbeladnen wähnten sie im Bruder,
Den Lässigen, den Schwächlichen –
Doch keiner rief: »Mein Bruder, wir sind alle schuldig!«
Nein, sie verhüllten psalmodierend ihre Köpfe
Und haßten sich.

3.

Der Krieg verjährte zum Gespenst,
Das zeitlos knöchern seine Finger
Um die willig-unfreiwill'gen Völker krallte.
Die Menschen taten von sich ihre Hüllen
Und sahn sich scheu voll Mißtraun an.
Ihr Haß ward müd, verschlackt.
Mit leeren Augen saßen sie beisammen.
Doch keiner war, der Bruder lächeln mochte
Und keiner, der den Andern weh in seine Arme schloß.
Gleichgültig blickten sie sich an und fremd.
Die Worte, die sie sprachen, waren Masken.
Sie wußten drum.
Sie hatten nicht die Kraft, in Einsamkeiten zu entfliehn
Und dort zu wappnen sich mit dem kristallnen Panzer.
So saßen sie beisammen
Mumien oder Grammophone.

PEOPLE

1.

When the war hit them like a mad dog
They screamed and shouted to each other
That they would fight together
And their will,
Like a wall of flames,
Would harden against the war.–
Or they did it just to survive,
Not to be alone
So unspeakably alone.

2.

Tremendous stones battered their souls.
They saw each other on the shoreless sea,
Drowning arms reaching out.
Felt agony tearing at their hearts.
They were wrong to blame their brothers,
The easygoing, the weak –
But no one called out: "No, we are all guilty!"
No, they covered their heads in psalms
And hated themselves.

3.

War was a specter
Who wrapped his timeless fingers
Round the willing and will-less.
The people shed their skin
And looked at each other shy, suspicious.
Their hatred grew tired and slagged.
With empty eyes they sat together.
No brother to crack a smile
And no one harmed another in his arms.
They looked at each other, indifferent and strrange.
The words they spoke were masks.
And they knew it.
They did not have the strength to withdraw in solitude
And wrap themselves in crystal armor.
So they sat together
Mummies or gramophones.

SOLDATEN

Ich kann die Gesichter meiner Kameraden nicht vergessen.
Sie ließen sich in Fabriken führen und zu Maschinenteilen pressen.
Vierjähriger Krieg hat ihre Seelen erdrückt und ihre Augen geblendet,
Das Menschliche ihrer Gesichter bespien, da starb es, geschändet.
Bei Dirnen aus dunklen Hafenschenken und schmutzigen Bordellen
Sieht man oft unter geschminkten Masken ein gütiges Lächeln quellen.
Aber die Gesichter meiner Kameraden gleichen erstarrten Lachen –
Gott! Bruder! Mensch! werden sie jemals wieder erwachen?!

DER KÖNIGLICHE MEISTERSCHUSS

Ein fortgejagter König schoß
(in seinem früheren Reich, versteht sich) Ehrenscheiben,
Worauf die Republik beschloß,
Nicht länger Republik zu bleiben.

AUSWENDIG LERNEN

Wir Männer, die wir nach fünf Jahren,
in denen wir – wir die Betrogenen waren,
heut zitternd vor Zorn den Haßschrieb gelesen,
der doch ihrer Blutschuld Beweis gewesen –

Wir Weiber, die wir, was wir geboren,
den Heimatlügnern vertrauend, in Schlachten verloren,
unsre Männer, unsre lieben Knaben
gemordet in der Erde liegen haben –

Wir Kinder, die wir vor Haßpoetenrichtern
stehen mit hungeralten Gesichtern,
vor Kerls, die unsre Händchen in Frondienst wollen zwingen,
den sie, zwei Mark die Zeile, in Stinnesblättern heilig singen –
Wir alle, wir alle, wir alle schwören
einen heiligen Schwur, und das Volk soll ihn hören,
wie's Freiheitslied ins Herz wir schmieden:
Wir wollen Frieden! Wir wollen Frieden!

Damit wir einst in helleren Tagen
die Otto und Börries zum Teufel jagen,
die sich wie Zecken in unsre Leiber krallten,
und die heute ihr schamloses Maul – nicht halten!

SOLDIERS

I can never forget the faces of my comrades.
They are guided into factories to man the machines.
Four years of war squeeze their souls to death, their eyes blinded.
Spit on what was human of their faces, where it died, defiled.
With whores out of dark harbor taverns and dirty brothels,
You can often see smiles welling up under their masks.
But the faces of my comrades are like laughter petrified –
God! Brother! Man! Will you ever wake again?!

THE ROYAL SHOT

A fleeing king, shot
(in his former kingdom, naturally) Sigils,
Whereof the republic decided
To no longer remain a republic.

WE REMEMBER

We men, we who after five years
were betrayed, today
we tremble with anger as we read the malediction
which proves the guilt of their blood –

We women, who we, what we have borne,
trusting in the homes we lost in battles,
our men, our dear boys
murded, lying in the ground –

We children who stand with hungry faces
before the poet-judges of hate,
men who want to force us into slavery
which they, for two marks on a sheet, call holy –
We all, we all, we are swear
a sacred vow, and the people should hear it
likea song of freedom smelt to the heart
We want freedom! We want freedom!

Once on brighter days
We'd drive Otto and Börries to the devil,
clinging to our bodies like ticks
and who today – can't shut their shameless mouths!

DIE FEUER-KANTATE

I

Ein altes Sprichwort

Du sollst nicht mit dem Feuer spielen,
sagt ein altes Sprichwort.
Wer mit dem Feuer spielt,
verbrennt sich die Hände.
Doch spielen viele Menschen
gerne mit dem Feuer.
Auch verbrennen Mörder
zuweilen ihre Opfer,
um die Spuren
des Mordes zu verwischen.

II

Das Hakenkreuz

Die Sonne brennt
seit Millionen Jahren;
ihr Feuer erwärmt
die frierende Erde,
das Getier in den Wäldern,
die Fische im Wasser
und die sanften Blumen.
Die Menschen lobten das
himmlische Feuer
und schufen sich
ein irdisches Bild
der kreisenden Sonne:
das Hakenkreuz.
Als über Deutschland
das Hakenkreuz zu leuchten
begann,
war es ein trübes Leuchten,
und es war ein Geruch
von versengtem
Menschenfleisch.

III

Die bösen Kommunisten

Warum brennt unsere Sonne,
warum leuchtet sie nicht?
sagten die Männer,
die das Hakenkreuz

THE FIRE-CANTATA

I

An Old Saying

You shouldn't play with fire,
says an old proverb.
Who plays with fire
burns their hands.
Yet many people glady
play with fire.
Murderers too will burn
their victims
to cover any trace
of their murder.

II

The Swastika

The sun has burned
for millions of years;
her fire warms
the freezing earth,
animals in the woods
fish in the water
and the gentle flowers.
People praised
the heavenly fire
and shaped
an earthly image
circling the sun:
the swastika.
As the swastika
began to shine
over Germany
it was a dull light,
with the smell
of scorched
flesh.

III

The Evil Communists

Why's the sun burning?
Why won't it shine?
ask the men
who wear swastikas

am Armband trugen.
Daran sind die bösen
Kommunisten schuld,
sie spielen nicht mit dem Feuer –
da liegt der Hund begraben.

IV

Beratung

Es war ein Streiten und Raufen,
welches Haus am
rötesten brennen würde
in der mondlosen Winternacht.
Und sie beschlossen,
den Reichstag anzuzünden.
Dort schlief die deutsche Freiheit
einen schweren traumlosen Schlaf.

V

Feurio

Der Reichstag brennt!
schrien die Extrablätter,
Der Reichstag brennt!
funkten die Morseapparate.
Der Reichstag brennt!
gröhlte das Radio.
Die bösen Kommunisten
haben mit dem Feuer gespielt,
das sollen sie büßen!
In dieser Nacht
verhafteten die Führer,
die das Hakenkreuz trugen,
Männer und Frauen
zu tausenden,
und sie wachten darüber,
daß die Feuerwehr
den Brand nicht lösche.

VI

Die Sonne

bringt es an den Tag
Als am nächsten Tag
die Sonne den Himmel rötete,
sah man verkohlte Balken
und einen Haufen Asche –
aber auch die Spuren
der Brandstifter.
Und die Menschen deuteten
mit Fingern auf ihre

on their armbands
Of course! The evil
communists are to blame,
they don't play with the fire –
a dog is buried beneath it.

IV

Council

There was fighting and quarreling
as to which house
would burn the reddest
in the moonless winter night.
So they decided
to set fire to the Reichstag.
German freedom was sleeping there,
a heavy, dreamless sleep.

V

Fire

The Reichstag burns!
the newspapers scream,
The Reichstag burns!
the telegram cries,
The Reichstag burns!
the radio roars.
The evil communists
have played with fire,
they must pay!
On that night
leaders wearing swastikas
were arrested,
Men and women
in the thousands
watched so that
the firemen couldn't
put out the fire

VI

The Sun

brings the day
And on the next day
the sun reds the sky,
one saw charred beams
a pile of ashes –
and the traces
of arson.
And the people
pointed their fingers

versengten Hände,
und es ging ein Flüstern
und Raunen
durch die Welt:
Hakenkreuz verbrennt
den Reichstag!

VII

Das Wunder

Wunder geschehen nicht
auf dieser Erde:
hast du ein Feuer erstickt,
und war es noch so
gewaltig,
kannst du es nicht mehr
entfachen
mit dem Atem
deines Mundes
oder
einem Blasebalg;
der Weise bedenkt,
bevor er
handelt.
Aber diesmal geschah
ein Wunder:
der Reichstag
brannte in einer Nacht –
doch er brennt,
brennt fort
in allen Nächten,
und er leuchtet
künftigen Geschlechtern!
Denn du sollst nicht
mit dem Feuer spielen.

at their
scorched hands,
and there a whisper
murmurated
through the world:
The swastika burnt
the Reichstag!

VII

The Miracle

Miracles don't happen
on this earth:
have you smothered a fire
and seen it burn still,
thundering,,
you can no longer
kindle it
with the breath
of your mouth
or a bellows;
the wise man thinks
before he
acts.
But this time,
a miracle:
The Reichstag
burned in a night –
and it burns
burns away
through all nights,
and it shines for
future generations!
That you shouldn't
play with the fire.

LUMPENLIED

Was fragt Ihr mich, woher ich kam
und wo meine Seele zerrissen.
Warum mein Körper hell fiebernd Blut
und meine Kleider verschlissen.
Sauft Ihr Tölpel und singt das Lied
vom Narren, der zur Heimat zieht.
Drob lachte selbst der Dreckspatz Tod
er rief herbei die Sippen
und klapperte mit seinen sieben
sieben Klapperrippen
Klipp Klapp.

Sei's drum wir trinken Brüderschaft
Ihr Knechte und Vasallen
Und haut man uns den Hintern voll
Wollen wir ... die Fäuste ballen.
Sauft Ihr Tölpel und singt das Lied
vom Narren, der zur Heimat zieht.
Drob lachte selbst der Dreckspatz Tod
er rief herbei die Sippen
und klapperte mit seinen sieben
sieben Klapperrippen
Klipp, Klapp.

LUMPENLYRIC

Why do you ask me where I come from
and where my soul's been torn.
Why my body's bright fevered blood
and my clothes were worn.
Drink yourself drunk and sing the lay
of the fool who drags himself home.
Even the shitsparrow of death laughed
and called the clans over
and rattled his seven
seven cracking ribs
Crick, crack.

So let us drink to brotherhood
You serfs and vassals
Our asses smashed
We want to . . . clench our fists.
Drink til we're drunk and sing the lay
of the fool who drags himself home.
Even the bastard of death laughs
and calls the clans over
and rattles his seven
seven crackling ribs
Crick, crack.

LIEBE

Ich bin das A und das O,
Der Anfang und das Ende.
Ich lege meine starken Hände
Auf Dein blasses, blütenbeschwertes Haar.
Mein Lachen
An frühlingsschwangeren Tagen
Klingt in Dir fort ....
Und Lieder ertönen
In Deiner lichterfüllten
Sehnsuchtsgestillten
Brust.
Mein Leid
Zerreißt mit schrillen Peitschenhieben
Den duftigen Schleier
Aus glitzernden Sonnenfäden und Tautränen,
Die zischend zerstieben –
Und giftiger Atem
Verpestet
Die Luft.
Ich bin der Sturm
Ich Dein Verlangen
Ich reiße Dich zu Boden
Durch heiße Begierde.
Ich trage Dich empor
Auf schönheitstrunkenen Blicken
Ins Unendliche . . . .
Und Deine Seele
Wird eins mit mir. –
Ich bin das A und das O.
Der Anfang und das Ende.

LOVE

I am the A and the O,
The beginning and the end.
I lay my hands
On your pale blossom-heavy hair.
My laughter
On springpregnant days
Resounds in you ....
And songs echo
In your lightfilled
Yearning-stilled
Chest.
With shrill lashes
My sorrow tears through
The fragrant veil
Of glittering sunthreads and dewtears
That hiss and disperse. —
And poisonous breath
Pollutes
The Air
I am the storm,
Your desire
I tear you to the ground
in fiery longing.
I carry you up
Toward infinity
With drunken sights of beauty. . . .
And your soul
Becomes one with me. –
I am the A and the O,
The beginning and the end.

UMARMUNG

Du kamst zu mir in farbigen Gewändern,
Dein Auge strahlte auf als Gotendom,
Dein Atem wob Gewölb aus Strahlenbändern,
Dein Schreiten glich verhaltnem Strom.
Und deine Hüllen glitten Dir zu Füssen,
Da standst Du vor mir, Schwester, lichtgereckt.
Ich senkte stumm die Stirn, um Dich zu grüssen,
Wie Sommerhauch, der Rosenknospen weckt.
Zwei fromme Menschen, die sich liebend ehren,
So strömten unsre Leiber in geahnten Quell,
Wir fühlten Lebensfülle fruchtgeschwellt sich mehren,
Lichtbündel sprühten um uns rot und hell.
Und als wir lächelten in Abschiedsneigen,
War Tanz in uns und süsser Töne Reigen.

STÄNDCHEN

Weiss nicht Mädel, sinds die grauen
Augen voll Verheißung und den sinnlich kühlen
Locken aller rätselhaften Frauen?
Ist der Duft, der strömt aus deinen Hüllen
der mein Sinnen mit den Düften
Märchenhafter Gärten kosend, küssend,
trunken will erfüllen?
Singt der Rhythmus deiner birkenschlanken Glieder,
meines Blutes toll berauschte Lieder?
Wünsche sind, die wie mystisch kultendunkle Schlangen
neu erwecken Lebensliebesglutverlangen.
– Oder will ein Teufel Possen mit mir spielen,
soll ich melancholisch hypochondrisch
nach des Weibes Beinen schielen?

EMBRACE

You came to me in colorful robes,
Eyes shining like a gothic cathedral,
Your breath wove vaulting ribbons of light,
Your step resembled a restrained current.
And your clothes slid to your feet,
There you stood before me, sister, lightdrenched.
I bowed my head in muted greeting,
Like a summer's breath to waken the roses buds.
Two pious people, honoring one another through love,
So our bodies flowed into a hidden river,
We felt the swell of ripening life ,
Bundles of light sparking red and bright around us.
And as we smiled in our nods goodbye,
There was dancing in us, sweet sounds going round.

SERENADE

Girl, I'm not sure, if it's the gray
Eyes full of promise and cool sensuality,
The lure of all enigmatic women.
Is it the scent that streams off your clothes
which fills my senses with the scents of
fairy-tale gardens, cuddling, kissing,
drinking til we're full?
Is the rhtyhm of your birchslender limbs
singing the mad songs of my intoxicated blood?
There are wishes which like mystic snakes
wake to a new desire for love and life.
— Or does a devil playing want to play with me,
should I, like a melancholic hypocondriac,
squint at the woman's legs?

RESIGNATION

Da sich dein Leib erschloss wie junger Frühlingsmorgen,
Und Deine Seele sich entfaltete im duftopalnen Tau,
Da Du Maria warst und Traum der Lieben Frau,
Und Venus hell in Sinnenlust geborgen.
Da sich Dein Schoss mir öffnete, auf daß ich strömend ihn erfülle,
Floh ich Erschreckter Dich und lief in regnerische Nacht.
Ich habe mich im tausendfachen Hohn verlacht,
Ich war Dir fern und fremd und nichts als Hülle.
Nun brach aus mir ein Quell von reifer Sommerglut.
Wie Strom in rauschend Meer möcht er in Deine Fülle münden,
Doch ach! Ein herbstlich schwarzer Schatten wuchs in Deinem Blut.
Oh dass ich glühe, während Deine Augen Müdes künden.
Denn Du gingst weiter, weintest wohl die nächtgen Stunden,
Und hast mit toten Dingen müd Dich abgefunden.

DIE HÄSSLICHE

1.

Mir graut vor meinem verkrüppelten Körper.
Ich ziehe hässliche Kleider an.
Wenn ich nach einem schönen Gewand greife,
Muss ich schrill auflachen,
Wie ein Humorist in einem Varieté,
Der dumme Couplets singt
Vor blöden Gesichten,
Und der sich erinnert,
Daß er einstmals mit seinem Blute
Flammende Verse geschrieben. —
Darum ziehe ich hässliche Kleider an.

2.

Ich bin meiner Seele müde.
Einst liess sie mich glauben,
Dass sie strahlte ein geschliffener Diamant,
Dass sie die körperliche Form in tausend Strahlen bräche,
Um meine flache Brust Gloriolen winde –
Doch wenn ich mich in den Augen des Mannes sah,
Den ich liebte,
Dann schaute mich meine Seele an,
Wie eine fahle, trübe Dämmerstunde ...

RESIGNATION

As your body opened like a young spring morning
And your soul unfolded in opal-scented dew,
Since you were Maria the dream of the Our Lady,
And held Venus in your bright sensuality.
As you opened to me I ran from you
Out into the rainy night.
I laughed at myself a thousandfold in scorn,
I was far and foreign from you and nothing but a shell.
A stream of summer's heat burst from me.
Like a river rushing into the sea it wants to meet your fullness,
But alas! A shadow of black autumn swelled in your blood.
Oh that I'd glow while your eyes speak of exhaustion.
But you went further, might have cried through the night,
And have wearily come to terms with dead things.

THE UGLY

1.

I dread my deformed body.
I put on ugly clothes.
When I reach for a beautiful garment
I have to burst out laughing
Like a vaudeville comedian
Singing stupid couplets
To stupid faces
And who remembers
That he had once written
Flaming verse in his blood.—
Thus I must put on these ugly clothes.

2.

I'm tired of my soul.
Once it led me to believe
That it shone like a polished diamond
Whose physical form would collapse into a thousand rays,
Halos streaming from my wounded chest —
But when I saw myself in the eys of the man
I loved,
My sould would gaze back at me,
Like a pale, hazy twilit hour.

3.

Ich will kein Kind gebären.
Einst ging ich mit wiegenden Schritten
Die Strasse entlang
Und mühte mich, es einer Dirne gleich zu tun.
Aber niemand kam zu mir.
Käme heute jemand, ich wiese ihm die Tür.
Ich bin zu wund, um ein Kind zu gebären.
Ich würde meinem Kinde Müdigkeit ins Blut schütten,
Aus meinen Liedern zuckte Enttäuschung.
Dann würde es kränkeln und ohne Kraft sein
Und mich hassen.

4.

Warum gehe ich nicht davon?
Ich bin nicht schwach.
Nur müde.
Und so werde ich noch viele Jahre
In meinem Zimmer sitzen
Mit den roten Plüschmöbeln
Und die Vasen anstarren,
Die meinem Auge wehe tun,
Und die Öldrucke.
Denn ich scheue mich, sie fort zu tun.
Sie alle gleichen mir.

[ICH SUCHE DICH]

Ich suche Dich.
Verflogen der Rausch von Sinnenlust,
Zerflattert die Lüge, die unbewusst
In meinem Herzen sich barg,
Ich suchte Dich unter frühlingsjungen Weibern
Mit sehnenden Blicken und schämigen Leibern
Und fand Dich nicht.
Ich ging zu liebessatten reifen Frauen,
Ich hoffte ihr Inneres zu schauen.
Und sah eine Kruste von Lüge und Schein
Und spielerisches Müdesein.
Da schlich ich zu jenen, die Liebe verkaufen
Ich gab ihnen Gold
Und sie kamen gelaufen

3.

I don't want to bear a child.
Once I walked down the street
With swinging hips
And struggled to do it like a prostitute.
But no one came to me.
If someone came today, I'd show him the door.
I am too sore to bear a child.
Childhood frustration spilling into my blood,
My songs shrugging with dissapointment.
The child would become sick and weak and
And hate me.

4.

Why don't I just leave?
I'm not weak.
Just tired.
And so I'll sit in my room
For many years
With this plush red furniture
And stare at the vases
And the oil paintingsThat hurt my eyes.
But I'm afraid to look away.
They all resemble me.

[I'M SEEKING YOU]

I'm seeking you.
Drunken sensuality has passed,
The lie that hid in my hear
Has fluttered away.
I sought you among springyoung women
With looks of longing and bodies of shame
And couldn't find you.
I went to mature women full of love
And hoped to see their interior.
I saw but a crust of lies and mere appearanceces
And playful ehxuastion.
So I snuck to the ones who sell love,
I gave them gold
And they came running

Und .... ich fand der Seele Sarg.
Ich suche Dich ...
Ich will Dich finden
Und müsst ich mit Ketten Dich binden.
Ich will Dich erkämpfen mit meinem Leben
Ich will Dich ertrotzen und mich Dir geben.
Ich will in Demut mich vor Dir neigen
und alle Wünsche sollen schweigen.
Wo bist Du,
Dass ich Dich schmücke königlich?
Ich suche Dich.

[STEHT EINE WACHT IN FRANKREICH]

Steht eine Wacht in Frankreich.
Die eint nicht Hass, die eint nicht Gier,
Ein Volk in seiner Liebe
siehst du erwecket hier.
Will keinen Ruhm, will keinen Stein,
Arbeit und Pflicht, so Tag um Tag.
Kein brausender Fanfarenklang;
eines Volkes beseelter Tiefensang:
Denkt an beschwornen Händeschlag.
Nicht Kreuze, Lied und bunte Ehr.
Es will sein Recht, es will sein Recht
nicht mehr.

GEBET AN MARIA (1915)

Weiße Blüten bring ich dir,
Maria.
Eine weiße Blüte war mein Kind,
Fielen Sonnensterne auf sein Haupt,
Kam in seine Augen leises Flimmern,
Wie die weißen Blüten still sich neigen,
Wenn der Maienwind sie sanft bewegt.
Da er von mir zog, und ich ihn küsste,
Fühlte ich in meinen Küssen herbstlich Frösteln,
Dass ich tief erschrak, er könnt erfrieren ...

AndI found the soul a coffin.
I'm searching for you . . .
I want to find you
Even if I have to bind you with chains.
I will fight for you with my life
I will defy you and give myself to you.
I will bow to you in humility
When all wishes sink silent.
Where are you
That I may royally adorn you?
I'm seeking you.

[THERE STANDS A WATCH IN FRANCE]

There stands a watch in France.
United by neither hate nor greed,
But a people
woken in their love.
They don't want fame or monuments,
but work and duty, day after day.
No wuthering fanfare,
but the soul of a people's song.
Think of hands congealed in oath.
Not crosses, songs, no honor.
It wants justice, justice
and nothing more.

PRAYER FOR MARIA (1915)

I'll bring you white blossoms,
Maria.
One of them was my child,
Starfish fell on his head,
A faint flicker came into his eyes
Like white blossoms bowing down,
Sofly stirring on the winds of may.
As he drew away from me and I kissed him
I felt autumnal chills in my kisses,
And I was deeply afraid that he might die of this cold.

FRÜHLING 1915
(R.D. IN VEREHRUNG)

Im Frühling zieh ich in den Kampf
Zum Siegen oder Sterben.
Was schert mich eigner Sorgen Krampf
Heut schlag ich ihn lachend in Scherben.

Im brausenden Sturm, mit lockigem Haar
reckt jauchzend ein Bub sich auf Erden:
Wacht auf, wacht auf, tot ist, was war,
wacht auf zu neuem Werden.

Ihr Brüder, wisst im Sturmwind kam
der junge Frühling fahren,
werft hurtig von Euch müden Gram
und zieht ihm nach in Scharen.

Noch nie hab ich es so gefühlt
wie ich Dich, Deutschland liebe,
Da Frühlingszauber Dich umspielt
inmitten Kampfgetriebe.

Im Frühling zieh ich in den Kampf
Zum Siegen oder Sterben.
Was schert mich eigner Sorgen Krampf
heut schlag ich ihn lachend in Scherben.

GEDENKT DES WORTS

Aus den Erläuterungen des Bundesrats zum Gesetz über den Vaterländischen Hilfsdienst: »Im Vaterländischen Dienst, welcher Art er auch sei, gibt es nicht Klassen und Schichten, sondern nur Staatsbürger.«

Gedenkt des Worts.
Schreibt es an Mauern, Türen, Wände.
Schreibts an Altäre, steingeformt.
Setzt erzne Tafeln, es zu künden.
In Parlamenten sei es heilges Gold.
Grabts in die Herzen, lasst es zünden,
und flammen nie erlöschend drin,

SPRING 1915
(IN HONOR OF R.D.)

In the spring I'm called to battle,
unto victory or death
What do I care for the weight of my worries?
Today, my laughter will tear him to shreds.

In a thundering storm a curly haired boy
stretches out on the earth, rejoicing.
Wake up, wake up; what once was is dead,
wake up to a new becoming.

Oh brothers, know that young spring
drove in on a tempest,
cast off your misery
and follow it in droves.

Never have I felt this way before,
how I love you, Germany,
as the magic of spring swirls about you
in the midst of all your army gear.

In the spring I'm called to battle,
to victory or death
What do I care for the weight of my worries?
Today, my laughter will tear him to shreds.

REMEMBER THESE WORDS

From the Bundesrat's report on the law regarding a draft of mandatory service for the Fatherland: "In the service of the Fatherland, no matter one's capacity, there are neither distinctions of class nor status: there are only citizens of the state."

Remember these words.
Write it all over doors, walls,
Write it on stone-cut alters.
Erect panels to announce it.
On sacred gold letters in parliament.
Graft it onto their hearts,
Let it burst into undying flames,

der Ohnmachtzorn, er sei zerschunden,
gebt Euer Letztes freudig hin.
Sprengt, was uns zweifelnd einst gebunden.
Gedenkt des Worts: Tut Eure Pflicht!
Doch, wenn des Friedens Lichter tagen,
der Alltag Euch in Unrecht zwängt,
dann fort mit allem Stank und Klagen,
fort mit dem Knecht, der Karren müde zog.
Gedenkt des Worts!
Und fordert ein den Schwur
Und handelt, wenn man Euch betrog!

GLOCKEN IM FELD

Des Abends, wenn violette Lichter
Über Feldern und Tannen spielen,
Der Sonne Purpurgold gehärtete Gesichter
Verklärt und stolze Arbeitsschwielen ...
Hör ich die abgerissnen Töne ferner Glocken.
Sie tauchen auf – verstummen – klingen ...
Wie Frauenhände fremde Vögel locken,
Die meiner Jugend Lieder singen.
Ein Gleiten ist in mir, ein Sehnen, Sich-Vermählen;
Das Krachen der Geschütze wird zu meines Blutes Wellen,
Die meinen jungen Leib wie Feuer quälen
Und jenes süsse, ferne Tönen übergellen.

SÄMANN – SOLDAT

Fremde Scholl durchpflügst Du mit starker Faust
Der braunen Erde zwingst Du Fruchtbarkeit.
Die Pferde ziehen Schritt für Schritt den Pflug,
die Pferde hängen ...
Und Du denkst an Weib und Kind
an deinen deutschen Herd.
In deinem Blick ist Liebe, die streift über fremdes Land.
Der Bauer wo mag der sein?
Hält ihn die Erde, die er Jahr um Jahr bebaut?
Kämpft er gegen dich mit Hass und Bitterkeit ...
Hüh, Schwarzer, zieh!

Cast off your impotence,
Eagerly give yourself unto the last.
What once bound us has crumbled in doubt.
Remember the words: Do your duty!
But when the lights of joy rises
and the quotidian again ensnares you,
then away with all your grumbling complaints,
away with the servant who wearily pulls the cart.
Remember the words!
And demand fulfillment of the oath:
Demand action when you are betrayed!

BELLS IN THE FIELD

On evenings when violet lights
Play over fields and fir trees,
Faces hardened by the sun's purple-gold
Corns and calluses from their proud work ...
I hear the severed tones of distant bells.
They appear — sink silent — reemerge . . .
Like the hands of women attracting strange birds
That sing the songs of my youth.
A gliding is in me, a longing to marry;
The crack of guns turns to waves in my blood
That vex my body like fire
And glide over those sweet, distant souds.

SOWER – SOLDIER

You plow through foreign soil with a strong fist,
forcing fertility unto the brown earth.
The horses pull the plow step by step,
The horses hang fire ...
You think of your wife and child
by your German hearth.
In your eyes love streams over foreign soil.
Where is the farmer?
Does the earth embrace him, which he toils year after year?
Does he struggle against you with hate and bitterness ...
Hey, Negro, pull!

DER SEELENTÄNZER

Ich tanze mit meiner Seele
Einen leichtbeschwingten Tanz.
Meine Füsse winden Schritte
Zu wellendem Sternenkranz.
Der Grund, auf dem ich tanze
Gedüngt mit Menschenleid.
Ich singe lächelnde Lieder
Erträumter Unendlichkeit.
Ich tanze durch dunkle Gewölbe,
Ich tanz über blühenden Wald,
Und halte ich rastend inne,
Ein feines Tönen erschallt!
Das war wohl meine Seele
Die da so silbern klang –
Oder war es nur die Erdnot
Die wie ein Glöckchen zersprang?

SYLVESTER 1916

Eine Fratze grinst mich grünlich an.
Höhnt: Nur Mut, ich bin das neue Jahr.
Packt das Leben, sei ein Mann.
Donnert: Fluch dem Gott, der mich gebar.

AM GRENZSEE

An Stacheldrahtverhauen
Verblutet Erde.
An Pfählen eingerammt in Fluten
Wie Speere durch Leiber geweihter Männer
Vermodert der See.
Seuche eitert in Hirnen.
Gott!

SOULDANCER

I dance a lighthearted dance
With my soul
My feet are winding steps
Toward an undulating circle of stars.
The ground on which I dance
Is fertilized with suffering.
I sing smiling songs
of dreamy infinity.
I dance through vaulting darkness
Dance over blooming forests,
And I pause to rest as
A fine tone rings out!
It was probably my soul
That sounded there so silverly –
Or was it just the earth
That shattered like a bell.

SYLVESTER 1916

A grotesque grimace greenly grins at me.
It scoffs: Be brave, I am the new year.
Seize the day, be a man.
It thunders: Fuck the god that bore me.

THE LAKE ON THE BORDER

The earth bleeds,
caught in barbed wire.
The rotting lake, spears
As though through the bodies
Of holy men.
Pestilence festers in the brain.
God!

EPISODE ZWISCHEN DEN GRÄBEN

Feldsoldat im letzten Jahr erschossen,
hat den Tod genug genossen.
Zieht den Spiegel aus der Hose;
Wasenkalk bespritzte Züge.
Murmelt düster: Leib ist Lüge.
Kalk ist Wahrheit, riecht wie Rose.

NACHT IM PRIESTERWALD

Der Vollmond fließt azurne Ströme
Um Bäume, die zerfetzt zerschossen,
Wie Krüppel stumm in sich verkriechen,
Von Schreckmorästen zäh umgossen.
Er deckt die Blöße wunder Zweige,
Die Blut und Eiter klebrig rinnen,
Mit gleißend kühlen Zitterhänden,
Gewebt aus feinstem Silberlinnen.
In Stunden, da das Blutmeer brandet,
Zerreißt Gestöhn die Tränenfülle:
Entsetzensschrei vor Gott und Menschen
Ächzt wurzellos durch nächtge Stille.

DER MEISTER
(NACH ELSE LASKER-SCHÜLER)

Wie er daherschreitet
Germanischer junger Priester
Im röckebesetzten Hörsaal
Zwei Ruhmbänder schmuckzieren
An seinem Brennesselrock.
Seine Augen küssen Blaustrümpfe hold
Wie er getagbucht aufstrebt.
Immer bringen seine Lippen
Centralfeurige Glut.
Seine Worte schreiten nur über Grund.
(Stolpern nie über Tiefe)
Wie er kunstverhalten ist.
Aus jedem Vortrag, den er hält
purpurt gläsernes Herz ...
nicht ...

EPISODE BETWEEN TRENCHES

A soldier shot in the field last year
has enjoyed death enough.
He pulls a mirror from his pants,
his face is streaked with lime.
Darkly murmurs: the body is lie.
Lime is truth, smells like roses.

NIGHT IN THE BOIS-LE-PRÊTRE

Azure rivers stream from the full moon
Over trees, shot to shreds,
Holing up inside themselves like cripples, silent
Swamps pour their shock in streams of mist.
He covers the nakedness of wounded branches
With sticky blood and glistening pus
Running cooly over his cool trembling hands,
Woven from the finest silver linen.
On the hours when the bloodsea breaks
It groans and rips the fullness of tears apart:
A scream of terror vor before God and man
Howls rootless through the silence of night.

THE MASTER
(AFTER ELSE LASKER-SCHÜLER)

Look how the young
Germanic priest paces
In the skirt-adorned lecture hall
His nettle dress bejewled
By two beautiful bands.
How his eyes gently kiss their bluestockings
Rearing up diaried on his podium.
His lips always
Glowing with innerembers.
His words merely glide over the surface.
(Never stumbling into the depths)
How he is pure aesthetics.
With every lecture he gives
his glass heart crimsons
not ...

BRIEF

Du Bruder in Russland schriebst
»Wir alle sind Kinder der Mühe,
Wir alle sind Kinder der Not
Dem Elend des Lebens glaubten wir
Durch Brudermorden zu entfliehn.
Die Schmach vergessen: sei unser heisser Wunsch
Und uns umarmen brüderlich: sei unser heißer Wille.«

Dank Bruder drüben.
Doch Du vergassest:
Wir Alle sind Kinder göttlichen Geistes,
Wir Alle Kinder der Fülle,
Unendlich reich.

Man konnte unsre Körper schänden
Doch unsre Seele können
Waffen nicht noch Gas vernichten.
Da sind wir Schützer.
Oder Feind. Wie wir's bestimmen.

Um unser Mensch-Sein geht es, Bruder.
Das ist viel.

DEM BRUDER

Du armer Mensch, der Du Gebete stammelst,
Zu jenem der am Kreuze qualvoll starb
In leidgekrümmten Händen Tränen sammelst
Ihn anflehst, der um Liebe warb.

Siehst nicht, daß Deine Lenden bluten
Von spitzen Eisen, durch Dein Fleisch gerammt,
Dass Deine Seele tränt, zerpeitscht von Ruten
Zu steter Unrast Du verdammt.

Dass Du gekreuzigt durch die Strassen schreitest
Einherschleppst mit Dir zähe Marterlast
Und während Du die Brust Dir weitest,
Dein Rücken tief sich beugt der schweren Last.

Du armer Mensch von soviel Schmerz gepeinigt
Sehnst Du den Ruf: Es ist vollbracht.
Sehnst, dass zerwühlter Geist gereinigt
Erleuchte sternenlose Nacht.

LETTER

My brother in Russia wrote
"We are all children of labor
We are all children of poverty
We thought we could escape
this misery of life through fratricide.
Our greatest wish: to forget our shame
Our ardent desire: to embrace our brothers."

Thank you, distant brother
But you forget:
We are all children of the holy spirit,
We are children of plenty,
Of infinite riches.

They can destroy our bodies
But weapons cannot
Destroy our souls, nor gas.
In this matter we are defenders;
Or enemies. It's up to us.

It comes down to our humanity, brother.
And that's a great deal.

DEAREST BROTHER

You poor man, stammering prayers
To someone who died agonizing on the cross,
Gathering tears in his crooked hands,
Beseeching He who advocated Love.

You cannot see that your loins are bleeding
From pointed iron rammed through your flesh,
That your soul is weeping, whipped raw
Damned to perpetual unrest.

That you walk crucified through the streets
Dragging your martydom with you,
And with each swelling of your chest
Your back balks low beneath this load.

You poor man, tormented by such pain
Longing for the call that it is done.
Longing that your tortured mind, once cleansed
May radiate through the starless night.

DEN SPIELERISCHEN

»Glaubst Du an Deines Landes Zukunft?
Glaubst Du, daß einst Dein Volk geeint,
Mit Schritten, ehern klingenden, marschiert,
Um sich das Reich zu schaffen, das ersehnte?
Glaubst Du es heute noch?
Entblößt sind alle hässlichen Instinkte,
Schamlos geht Mensch den Nächsten an,
Der Habsucht schmutziggrüne Zunge
Lechzt aus gespaltnem Maul,
Von Händen triefet Haß, die fromm sich straffen sollten!
Der Dichter spricht:
Dich trifft die Schuld, Du haust in Caféhäusern
Gebild aus spitzen Nadeln, die Verstandesschärfe eisig blinken.
Und turnst gleich Komödianten am erhöhten Reck,
Lässt Trommeln wirbeln, hei! Musik verstummen,
Um kühnen unerhörten »Geistsprung« zu jonglieren
So schaffst Du nie Gemeinschaft
Zur Gemeinschaft fehlt Dein Volk.

Du nahst dem Volk auf Wegen zweien falschen.
Der eine flucht ihm, sagt, es kann zerstören
Und sei zum Aufbau allzu plump.
eut ist es trüber Saft, doch morgen wird es gären.

Der andre hüllt es ein mit Glitzerflittern
In seinen Mantel wortbereiter Liebe,
Der Mantel ist zu dünn, er kann den Frierenden nicht wärmen,

Bevor nicht Blut den Acker düngt,
Bevor nicht Menschen Märtyrer geworden
Wegmeiler rot auflodernd in der Nacht
Bleibt Caféhaus der Ort, wo Euer Bach versandet.
Ich achte Euren Schwall gleich dem Geplärr
Steriler Weiber, die bei violetten Lichtern
Sich aufgeblasne Jahrmarkthähne krähend plustern.

Kennt ihr die Stadt mit ihren fiebernden Fabriken
Die Scheinpaläste Elefanten gleich erdrücken?
Haßt ländliche Natur, geht fremd vorbei am Farbenspiel
Nach Sonnenuntergang. Wart niemals innig
Hoch auf Bergesschroffen, wo schwielig Kiefer steilt,

TO THE PLAYFUL

»Do you believe in the future of your country?
Do you believe that once the people unite
Marching with steps the sound of iron
To bring about the world you long for?
Do you still believe in that?
All our ugly instincts are exposed,
Shamelessly one approaches the next
The dirty-green greed of their tongues
Dribbles from split lips,
Hate oozes from their hands, which should be bound in prayer!"
The poet speaks:
You carry the blame, you dwell in coffeehouses
Weaved with sharp needles, sagacity's icy blink.
You romp about like comedians on stage!
Let the drums thunder, hey! The music stops
To juggle bold, unheared-of "leaps of faith"
You don't create community like this
The people lack a binding glue.

You've approached them the wrong way.
One method curses them, says they can destroy
And are all too clumsy to build.
Today's juice is muddy, but tomorrow it'll ferment.

The other way wraps it up with glittery tinsel
In his coat of word-ready love,
But his coat is all too thin, how could it warm he who is freezing

Before blood fertilizes the field,
Before men become martyrs
Signal fires flare up red iacross the night
The café is where your river fizzles out.
I respect this flood like the babble of
Sterile women, who become crows
In the violet light, puffed up, cawing.

Do you know the city with its feverish factories?
Palace facades to hide the smothering of elephants.
The rural nature of hate streams past the
Playful colors of sunset. Never waits high
In the crags of mountains, where pinetrees gnarl and twine,

Den Stürmen, Schwarm von Panzerflugzeug, wehrt.

Merkt auf ich schreie gellend Weckruf!
Fühlt Ihr es nicht wie überall im Lande
Von Leid gebrochne Menschen auf Euch warten
Auf daß Ihr ihnen Keim seid, neu Sich zu gebären.
Kommt gross und stark mit einfachen Gebärden
Die künstlich spitzen Waffen dienen niemals Seelenkampf
Das Volk will Worte hören, aus Erschütterung gewachsen,
Und die Bereitschaft stetig flackernd zeugen.
Das Volk will Taten sehn, will aufgerüttelt sein
Durch Blut von Kämpfern der Idee, das rohe Macht verspritzte.

Lebt unterm Volk, befreit Persönlichkeiten

Dann wächst einst Tag aus pflugbezwungnem Boden
Dann rauschen Flügel in der Mittagsstunde
Gemeinschaft schwingt ihr Banner sturmgeschwellt.
Geballter Ruf, wie junger Mutter schmerzlichfroher Schrei
Verheisst Euch *Menschheitsbund*.

KRIEGSMETHODE
(KLEINE GESCHICHTE UNTER LOKALES ZU LESEN)

In roten Zuckerstückchen
Schwären Pestbazillen
Wer angelockt von sü.em Duft
Sie wohlig knirschend ißt
Siecht qualvoll hin

Menschen Europas
Bekämpften sich auf diese hohe Art
Im zwanzigsten Jahrhundert –

Ein Kind las es.
Und hängte sich auf.

Storms and swarms of aircraft stand defiant.

Listen! I'm screaming the alarm!
Can you not feel as though all the country
Is bent under the weight of suffering
And awaits your breath in kindling?
Come large and strong with simple gestures.
The artificial sharpness of blades never serve the soul in warfare,
They want to hear trembling words born from terror,
And their willingness shows on flickering faces
The people want to see action, want to be aroused
By the sacrificial blood of ideology, that spits raw power.

Live among people, liberated souls

One day emerges from plow-toiled soil,
Then wings rustling at noon
Collectivity waves its banner, stormswelled.
A cumulative cry, like the painful joyous cries of young women
Promises you the convenant of *humanity*..

METHODS OF WAR
(A LITTLE STORY TO READ IN THE LOCAL PAPERS)

A virus festers
In little red bits of sugar,
Attracting those with its sweet fragrance
To eat them with a delicious crunch
And waste away in agony.

The people of Europe
Fought one another in this grand manner
In the twentieth century—

A child read this.
And hanged himself.

[ICH WEISS UM DEINE TRÄNEN, BRUDER.]

1.
Ich weiss um Deine Tränen, Bruder.
Du streckst gedankenmüde Hände
Nach warmer Form voll süssem Duft,
Die Dir ein frohes Lächeln gab.
Du nanntest sie (und Deine Augen ruhten tief,
Als schautest Du in weite Ebne)
Ersehnte Heimat.
Da zischen schöngestaltet Menschen zähen Schleim
Und jagen geifernd Dich von dannen.

2.
Sei ruhig, Bruder, trockne Deine Tränen.
Sei Erdreich!
Baum!
Der in Dir wissend Wurzel schlägt.
Wohl tönst Du nicht in Farbenharmonien,
Zerzauste Kiefer, rissig trotzest Du dem Sturm.
Und trotzest jenen, die da wähnten,
Sie könnten Deine Wurzel, die wie zarte Fühler
Sich zuckend lösten, dorren machen.

DER HEILAND GEHT DURCH DIE VORSTADT

Frauen, die mit welkem Schoss
Welke Kinder in die dunklen Höfe schicken.
Männer, die nach dumpfem Los
Schweren Schrittes wandern in Fabriken.
Häuser, die Kasernen eins dem andern gleichen,
Mit gedrückten Stirnen müde sich gen Himmel schleichen.

Schluchzend streichelt er ein schmutzges Kind mit schinngen Haaren,
Sammelt um sich all die kleinen kümmerlichen Scharen.
Voll Erwartung schauen sie ihn fragend an,
Seltsam dünkt sie dieser fremde Mann.
Als er ihre Augen leer und hungrig sieht,
Möcht er ihnen Märchen singen oder auch ein frohes Lied.
Doch da beugt sich eins der Kleinen nieder in den Kot
Und es ruft mit Fistelstimme: »O da liegt ein Stückchen Brot!«
Und die andern stürzen gierig darauf los,
Dünne Ärmchen raufen sich; ach der Hunger ist so gross.

BROTHER UPROOTED

1.
I know of your tears, brother
You reach your thoughttired hands
Toward the form of warm, sweet air,
Which reflects your joyous smile.
You named her (your eyes in deep repose,
As though transfixed on a distant field)
The home you longed for.
Where beautifully molded clay people
Spat venom and chased you away.

2.
Be calm, brother, dry your tears.
Be as the soil!
As the tree
Which lays its roots in you, knowing full well.
And while you may not be tinged in the harmony of colors,
You windswept pine, cracking and weaving you brave the storm.
You defy all those who thought
They could dry out your roots which,
Twitch like tender antennae, had shed themselves for you.

OUR SAVIOR WALKS THROUGH THE SUBURBS

Women with withered wombs
Send withered children into dark courtyards.
Men and their bad fortune
Wander with lead steps into factories.
Houses resemble baracks, one and another alike,
Their furrowed eyebrows barely slink toward heaven.

Sobbing, he caresses a child's dirty hair
Which falls into small, miserable piles around him.
They look at him, questioning,
The strange man hardly notices them.
He wants to sing them a happy song of tell them fairy tales
When he sees their empty, hungry eyes.
But then one of the little ones bends down in the dirt
And calls out in a falsetto "Oh, there's a little piece of bread!"
And the others pounce,
Thin little arms struggling; there is such hunger.

Als ers sieht, da möcht er weinen, aber sein Gesicht wird hart,
Alles Licht beginnt zu schwelen, alles Mitleid grau erstarrt.
Kann nicht Vater! rufen und ergeben sich in ihn versenken.
Hohn scheint ihm die Lehre: einst wird ers zum Guten lenken.
Seine Fäuste ballen sich in tiefsten, niegewussten Nöten,
Trotzig bäumt er seine Seele: *Wo ist Gott? Ich will ihn töten!*

Seine Worte glühen blutge Fackeln in der Luft.
Und ihm ist, als sei er auferstanden aus verwester Gruft.

DER RUF
(NACH EINER STATUE VON FRITZ CLAUS)

Wir schreiten
In Demut
Unendliche Wege
Und wissen nicht,
Wohin.
Wir hören ein Klingen
In frohhellen Höhen
Das tönt wie kristallnes
Erdfremdes Lied. –
Wir schreiten entgegen
Dem quellenden Leben
Dem tanzenden Tode
Und schauen in Fernen
Die, Kinder, wir ahnten.

STUDENTINNEN

Die Frauen gehn mit Wünschen schwanger.
In Nächten bricht aus ihrem Mund ekstatisch Schrei:
»Erlöset uns vom dunklen Schmerzenspranger!
Gebt Kinder uns! Umarmt uns! Macht uns frei!
Voll Lust wolln wir das Kind gebären.
Das tiefste Wissen lehrt, dass wir ein Weib.
Mit unsrem Herzblut müssen wir ein Totes nähren –
Erfüllung wird durch fruchtbeladnen Leib.«

He wants to cry as he watches, but his face hardens
All the light begins to smolder, all compassion paralyzed.
He cannot Father! all his cries surrender and sink into him.
Those teachings sound like scorn: one day he will lead them to the Good.
His fists clenched in the deepest poverity he has ever known.
Defiant, the whole of his soul bellows: *Where is God? I'll kill him!*

His words glow like bloodred torches in the air.
It seems to him as though he has risen from a mouldering crypt.

THE CALL
(AFTER A STATUE BY FRITZ CLAUS)

We stride
In humility
Along infinite paths
And don't know
Where we're going.
We hear a ringing
Above in happy bright heights:
A crystalline,
Unearthly song.—
We stride against
This swelling life,
Toward dancing Death
And gaze into distances which,
Children, we felt.

STUDENTS

Women walk, pregnant with desire.
An ecstatic scream breaks from her mouth in the night:
"Release us from the dark gallows of pain!
Give us children! Embrace us! Set us free!
We would give birth with pleasure.
Our deepest knowledge tells us that we are women.
With our heart's blood we must nourish a death —
Only fulfilled by a fruit-laden body.

LEGENDE

Alte Sage geht von Frauen,
Die Kinder andrer Frauen töten.
Sie sind verdammt!
Zu Leben ohne Frucht verdammt.

Aus allen Fabriken der Welt,
In denen Kugeln geschmiedet,
Eisenhöhlen mit giftigen Gasen gefüllt,
Bomben mit augenätzenden Säuren
Tötgeschosse gedreht ...
Treten in wallenden Reihen
Bleiche Frauen.
Hände gleiten von eingefallenen Brüsten,
Decken kraftlos verwelkten Leib.
Lallen ein Lied ...
Wandern auf Landstrassen,
Knien nicht, fluchen nicht,
Wandern und
Lallen ein Lied.
Das lautet:
Ein Kind ...

Ein Kind ...

Der Teufel verwünschte ihr Lallen,
Das ihm Ohren ätzte,
Sich gelb um seine Augen legte wie giftiges Gas.
Bat den Gekreuzigten,
Mittler zu sein,
An Gottes Thron.
Gott möge die Frauen verdammen
Zu ewigem Schweigen und Feuerqual. –

Den Heiland fror.
Er dachte der Hungerkrallen, die viele Frauen gezwungen,
Er dachte des Kriegsgebots.
Aber dann schüttelte er sein Haupt
Und verhüllte es mit weissen Tüchern.

Jahre durch lallte der Frauen Lied.
Da schrie der Teufel grässlichen Fluch
Und schlich sich zum Vater.

LEGEND

An old tale about women
Who kill the children of other women.
They are damned!
Damned to live without fruit.

In all the factories of the world
Where bullets are forged
Iron casings filled with poisonous gases
Bombs filled with eye-eating acids
Spinnings projectiles of death ...
Pale women
Step forward into their ranks.
Hands sliding from drooping breasts
To cover their withering bodies.
Murmuring a song ...
Roaming on country roads
Not kneeling, not cursing,
Wandering and
Babbling a song.
That ends in:
A child ...

A child ...

The devil curses their babble
That etches into his ears,
Yellow around his eyes like poison gas.
He bid the crucidied
To intervene
On the throne of God.
God has damned women
To eternal silence and fire.

The savior shivered,
Thinking of the pangs of hunger that plagued many women,
Thinking of the treaties of war.
But then he shook his head
And covered it with a white cloth.

For years the women babbled on.
Then the devil lauched a dreadful curse
And slithered toward the father.

Gottes Fäuste krampften sich,
Dass in sein Fleisch die Nägel drangen
Und rote Bluttropfen fielen.
Mohnfelder wuchsen da.
Wer auf ihnen schlief, starb.
Dann stöhnte Er auf,
Dass die himmlischen Bäume
Zu zittern begannen
Und ihre Blätter drei Tage
Vertrocknet zu Boden hingen.
Geängstigt wollten die Engel ein Lied anstimmen ...
Da kreischten sie.
Als sie es merkten,
Liefen sie zur Madonna.

Maria starrte ins Leere
Und hielt die Hände weit ausgestreckt
Von ihrem gesegneten Leibe.
Ihr Gesicht war hart.
Alle Milde leuchtete auf Tränen,
In ihren gekrümmten Händen gesammelt.
Die hielt sie drum weit von sich gestreckt.

Und Gott hieß den Teufel gehen.

Durch Wüsten schritten die Frauen,
Lallten ihr Lied
Ein Kind ...
Ein Kind ...

Da hundert Jahre vergangen,
Tappten auf nackten rosigen Füssen
Die ungeborenen Kinder
Zur Jungfrau Marie,
Falteten fromm ihre Händchen

Maria lächelte

Und es hub im Himmel ein Schluchzen an
Wie eine wehe Melodie,
Die ruhelos verstörte Töne sammelt
Zu sanfter Harmonie.

Und Gott erlöste die Frauen.

God's fist were clenched so tight
That his nails pierced his skin
And red drops of blood fell to the ground.
Poppies grew there, and
Whoever slept there, died.
Then he groaned
So the heavenly trees
Began to tremble
And their dry leaves hung
Low for three days.
In fear the angels attempted to sing,
But only a scream was heard.
When they realized this
They ran to the Madonna.

Mary stared into space
And held her hands outstretched
From her blessed body.
Her face was hard.
All gentleness gleaming out
Of the tears gathered in her crooked hands
She held them far from her.

And God told the Devil to go to her.

The women walked through deserts
Babbling on:
A child ...
A child ...

When a hundred years went by
The unborn childen
Groped on rosy naked feet
Toward the Virgin Mary,
Folded their hands in piety.

Mary smiled

And a sobbing began in heaven
Like a painful melody,
Which gathers cacophony
Into gentle harmony.

And God redeemed the women.

Über ihren Gräbern wuchs
Cypressenhain.
Drin spielten junge Rehe.

DÄMMERUNG IM KERKER

Mit schweren Schleiern ist ihr Haupt umwunden,
In schwarzen Höhlen kettet sich der müde Blick,
Die Füsse schleppen, wie mit strengem Strick gebunden,
Unselge, wissend um ihr lastendes Geschick.
Die Lieder, die in grauen Kerkerwänden nisten,
Erheben flatternd sich zu traurigem Gesang,
Wie Stoppelfelder die bei trübem Regen Leben fristen
Begleitet ihre Schwermutsmelodie den abendlichen Gang.
Stumm wühlen die Gefangnen in zerquälten Ecken ...
Erinnerung erlischt, verkohlte Asche mordet heisse Glut.
Verweht das Tagesspiel mit Sommerrosenhecken –
Eintönig gurgelt über Erde graue Flut.

DER BESIEGTE

Er war so einsam, dass die blaugetünchten Wände,
Wie stumme Feinde höhnisch seinen matten Blicken wehrten.
Ihm schienen seine eignen fieberheissen Hände
Gleich fremden Pilgern, die sich stumm von dannen kehrten.

Zu grünlich weichen Raupen wurden ihm die Stunden.
Er hörte Melodien, die Wächter blechern, grausam um ihn standen.
Auf seinem Antlitz brachen auf unzählge Wunden,
Die roten Dornenkranz um seine Stirne wanden.

Da zog er seine Decke über sich. Begann zu sprechen:
»Nun überwind ich Gott. Ich hab den Tag zur milden Nacht geschaffen.
In hellem Lichte sollte ich in Einsamkeit zerbrechen.
Ich wehre mich. Mein Wille siegt. Noch sind mir Waffen.«

Er starb. Die Schwester kam mit sachlich kühlen Schritten.
Behutsam hob die Decke sie: Da stiegs empor wie Sonnenreigen. –
Doch niemand sah den letzten Kampf, den er gestritten,
Den Schmerz des Letztverhöhnten und sein bittres Schweigen.

And cypress groves grew
Over their graves,
Where young deer now play.

DUSK IN DUNGEONS

Their heads are wound with heavy veils,
Tired eyes shackled in black hollows
They drag their feet, as though bound with ropes,
The wretched of the earth know the fates that haunt them.
There are songs nesting in these gray dungeon walls,
Rising they flutter into sorrowful singing,
Their melancholy melody accompanies the passage of evening
Like fields of stubble that eke out a life in bleary rain
The prisoners writhe quietly in their tortuned corners ...
Memory fades just as charred ash replaces blazing embers.
Those games we played in the summer choke on the wind –
A monotonous gray tide gurgles over the earth.

THE VANQUISHED

He was so lonely, and the bluewashed walls
Repelled his gaze like silent enemies.
His own feverish hands seemed like estranged pilgrims
Who turned from him in silence.

The hours were soft, greenish caterpillars to him.
The wardens and their grim melody standing watch.
Countless wounds broke across his face,
Weaving a red crown of thorns about his forehead.

He pulled his blanket over him, gegan to speak:
"Now I conquer God. I've forged a soft night from the day.
I should've broken into loneliness in the bright light.
I will resist. My will shall prevail. These are my weapons."

He died. The sister came in on soft, dutiful steps.
Slowly she raised the blanket: It rose like the dancing of suns. –
And yet no one had seen the last battle he fought,
The pain of one scorned, the residue of bitter silence

DER FACKELTRÄGER

Ich trage schweigend die Fackel wie eine heilge Monstranz.
Doch niemand kniet nieder und betet den Rosenkranz,
Und niemand, der strömend sein Herz darbringt,
Und niemand, der hoffend O hilf uns! singt.

Unsichtbar leuchtet die himmlische Glut.
In weissen Perlen tropft göttliches Blut.
Ihr Glanz ist kristallen, wie nördliche Nacht.
Dem Blinden dünkt sie ein schwelender Schacht.

Der Geist glüht gefoltert, doch löscht ihn kein Sturm.
Die Körper verwesen, doch frisst ihn kein Wurm.
Er trotzet des Fallbeils, und trotzet des Schlags,
Er wartet des Wunders, er wartet des Tags.

Dem läuten die Glocken, dem reckt sich der Mann,
Dem schreitet entgegen, wer schreiten noch kann.
Dann trag ich nicht einsam die Fackel zum Tal
Und lösche der fiebernden Menschen Qual.

Dann wandert die Menschheit zum quellenden Licht.
Verfehmt ist die Sühne, verfehmt das Gericht!
Ein heiliges Glühen, ein heiliger Klang
Wird himmlisches Lächeln und heller Gesang. –

Ich trage schweigend die Fackel wie eine heilge Monstranz.
Doch niemand kniet nieder and betet den Rosenkranz
Und niemand, der strömend sein Herz darbringt,
Und niemand, der hoffend O hilf uns! singt.

ABEND IM MÄRZ

Die Buchen dunkeln gegen blassen Himmel
Der Zweige Kahlheit krümmt sich scheu and zag
Ermattet schlürft der Märzstrom durch die Strassen
Nun flattert Dämmrung blauen Flügelschlag.

In Träumerschritten ebbt des Tages Schwere
Versunken küßt das Auge nackten Baum,
Daß grauer Menschen Sehnen Frühling weckte
Zu buntem Leben zarten Knospensaum.

THE TORCHBEARER

In silence I carry the torch like a holy monstrance.
Yet there is nobody kneeling and reciting the rosary,
And nobody pouring their heart out,
And nobody hopefully singing "Oh help us!"

The embers of heaven shine unseen.
Divine blood dripping in white pearls.
Their crystalline glance like a northern night.
To the blind man it is but a smoldering shaft of light.

The spirt glows on the stocks, no storm to quench this.
Their bodies rot and no worms come to feast.
He defies the guillotine, he resists each blow.
He waits for a miracle, waits for the day.

The bells ring for him, a man stretches towards him,
Those who can still walk walk towards him.
I will no longer carry the torch alone
Down to the valley to end our suffering..

Humanity will swell toward the expanding light.
Atonement is banished, Judgement is outlawed!
A holy ember, a holy sound
Becomes a heavenly smile and a bright song. –

In silence I carry the torch like a holy monstrance.
Yet there is nobody kneeling and reciting the rosary,
And nobody pouring their heart out,
And nobody hopefully singing "Lord help us!"

AN EVENING IN MARCH

The beech trees darken against a pale sky
Bare branches bending, shy and timid
The current of March slurps through the streets, tired,
Now dusk flutters its blue wings.

The day's gravity ebbing back like the steps of a sleepwalker
The eyes sink in to kiss the naked trees.
Oh that gray people would wake yearning for spring
And the tender buds caressing the colors of life.

ABEND AM WELSSEE

Den Eichenwald umgittern lächelnd Birken
In schwärzlich blauem Wasser schattet Astgerank
Wie Japans Frauen seid'ne Blumen wirken
Umrahmt von purpurroter Wolkenbank.

Der Abendwind streift mild um reife Ähren
In sanfter Wellen Spiel verhaucht sein Kuss.
Aus blauen Glocken tönet schmerzliches Gewähren
Vom Walde hallt verrollend ferner Schuss.

Im Teich quarrt hohl der Frösche Zanken.
Die Grillen zirpen rührig spitzen Ton.
Am Ufer steht ein Knabe, schlank und nackt.

Und da er steilen Sprungs die Wellen packt
Quirlt Jubelschrei wie glutend roter Mohn.
Aufstrudeln Fluten, die das Wunder tranken.

WUNDER

Meine ruhelosen Hände
Die durch Raum and Zeiten zuckend weichen
Werden fromme stille Pilger,
Wenn sie Deine blasse Stirne streichen.

DEN IN DACHAU »STANDRECHTLICH« ERSCHOSSENEN ROTGARDISTEN

Fünf Rotgardisten wurden hier erschossen
Fünf Rotgardisten, die man »Verbrecher« nannte.
Namenlose, die kaum einer kannte –
Proletarierblut, heiliges Blut, ward vergossen.

Fünf Proletarier, durch einen Gedanken zusammengeschlossen
Revolutionäre Brüder und Kämpfer der Armen,
Überfallen und abgeurteilt ohne Erbarmen –
Proletarierblut heiliges Blut ward vergossen.

Dreißig gefangne Weißgardisten wurden nicht erschossen.
Man klärte sie auf und gab ihnen freies Geleite.
Arbeiter wie wir, betörte Brüder im Streite –
Proletarierblut heiliges Blut ward vergossen!

AN EVENING ON LAKE WELS

Birches smile as they fence the oaks in,
Their tangled branches casting shadows on the blackish blue water
Just as the women of Japan seem like silken flowers
Framed by a purple-red bank of clouds.

The gentle evening wind brushing through wheat fields
On soft waves, its breath a playful kiss.
A painful reminder streams from blue bells:
A distant shot comes echoing from the woods.

Frogs quarrel in the hollow pond.
The crickets chirp their harsh tone.
A boy stands on the bank, slender and naked.

And with a bold jump he grasps the waves,
A joyous cry like red poppies aglow.
A vortex bubbles up and swallows the miracle.

MIRACLE

My restless hands which roam
Twitching through time and space,
Become pious and silent pigrims
When they meet your pale forehead.

TO THE RED GUARDS EXECUTED "BY DECREE OF THE STATE" IN DACHAU

Five red guards were shot here,
Five red guards, you would call them "criminals."
Nameless, hardly anyone knew them –
Proleblood, holy blood, was shed.

Five proles united by a single thought,
Revolutionary brothers, fighters for the poor,
Ambushed and convicted without justice –
Proleblood holy blood was shed.

Thirty white guard prisoners were not shot.
They were given a pat on the back and given save passage.
Workers like us, tortured brothers in struggle –
Proleblood holy blood was shed!

ORGASMUS DER SOMMERNACHT

Zinnoberrote Träume wild emporreißt unterdrückte Lust.
Die wandgeketteten verdammten Pritschen stöhnen.
O nun erwachen Feste, die den kahlen Raum verschönen,
Ein dunkler Dämon wühlt in unsrer Brust.

O unser Biß in Frauenbrüste ist kein zartes Minnen.
Pucellen überfallen wir und trinken der Genossinnen erstes Blut,
Im Schoß der eignen Schwester unsre Wollust ruht,
Wir peitschen durch die Städte geile Bürgerinnen.

Und schmale Knaben sind uns gut. Sie schmiegen
Hingegeben den gelösten Leib an uns Verfehmte.
Sie werden heute Nacht bei allen Brüdern liegen,

Und keiner ist, der sich des Sträflings auf der Pritsche schämte.
Erwachend höhnen, Kupplerinnen, uns die Eisengitter.
Im Morgengrauen aber sind die Zellen wie verweinte Mütter.

GEFÄNGNIS UND ZEIT

Was ist ein Jahr und was ist eine Stunde
Im Acker Zeit, der brach zu unsern Füßen liegt

Einst war die Zeit wie eine seltsame Legende
Die in brokatnem Gewand das Wunder hüllte
Wir wußten, daß es köstlich uns erfüllte,
Wenn unsere Hand den goldenen Schlüssel fände

Nun tönt der Glockenschlag der Uhren toten Klang
Wir sind vertrieben aus dem Kreis der Zeit
Wir sind gestoßen in die antlitzlose Finsterheit.

Wie Nebelfetzen flattern wir im Käfiggang,
Von Wächteraugen spähenden bedrängt. –

A SUMMER NIGHT'S ORGASM

Wild vermillion dreams bubbling up from suppressed desire.
Damned beds chained to the wall, groaning.
O now the festivities begin, embellishing the room,
A dark demon digging into our breast.

O when we bite the breasts of women it's no tender love.
We decend on maids and drink the virgin blood of our comrades,
Our lust lingers in the lap of our very sisters,
We whip the horny bourgeoisie through the cities.

And the boys love us. They surrender
Their bodies to us, the wicked.
They will lie with all our brothers tonight,

And nobody is ashamed of this convict on his bed.
Upon waking, the iron bars – those matchmakers – scorn us.
But at dawn the cells are like tearstained mothers.

PRISON AND TIME

What is a year and what is an hour,
in the time of the field that lies fallow under our feet.

Time was once an curious tale
That kept its miracle folded under brocade garments.
We knew it would satisfy us, deliciously
If our hand could find the golden key.

Now the clocks strike death,
We are cast from the sphere of time
Thrust into the faceless dark.

Like shredded fog we flit through our caged corridors,
Weighed down by the heavy eyes of the warden. –

FÜR ERICH MÜHSAM
(FREI NACH ERICH MÜHSAM)

Es war einmal ein echter Intellektueller,
Ein eitler Intellektueller, ein schlechter Intellektueller
Der glaubte, er sei ein Prolet.
Er zückte wider die andern die Lanzen
Er dichtete Revoluzzerstanzen
Mit blechernem Phrasengeklirr.

Es war einmal ein richtiger Intellektueller,
Ein pfiffiger Intellektueller, ein nichtiger Intellektueller,
Von dem sagte der Proleter:
»Der springt wie die tollsten Soller Flöhe
Und glaubt, er springt in Proletenhöhe,

Und springt doch nur aktuell!«
Das hörte der »rein Intellektuelle«
Der Café-Intellektuelle, der Kain-Intellektuelle,
Kniff ein den ummähnten Schwanz
»Verdorben seid Ihr, verfluchte Proleten
(sprach er) von den verdammten Moneten
Pfui Teufel, Ihr Knechtepack!

Ihr seid gemauserte Intellektuelle,
November-Intellektuelle, verlauserte Intellektuelle,
Ich einzig blieb Proleter,
Ich setz mir ein Denkmal aus Revoluzzerbronze,
Ich pfeif auf Euer Bonzengegronze,
Ihr seid nicht mehr kompetent.«

So schrie der entmannte Intellektuelle,
Der entlarvte Intellektuelle, der verrannte Intellektuelle,
Schwur blutige Rache dem Volk.
Da lachte kräftig der echte Prolete
Und sagte »Schmück Du als Denkmal die Städte,
Die Du als Politikaster versaut!«

FOR ERICH MÜHSAM
(ADAPTED FROM ERICH MÜHSAM)

There was once a real intellectual
A vain intellectual, a shoddy intellectual,
Who believed he was a prole.
He drew his sword against the others,
Penned revolutionary verse
With the tinny clang of clichéd phrases.

There was once a true intellectual,
An acute intellectual, an inane intellectual,
And the workers said,
"He jumps like the craziest fleas in debt
And thought he was reaching proletarian heights,

But he is jumping with the times!"
The *absolute intellectual* heard this
The café-intellectual, the Kain-intellectual
Whipped their tails between their legs
»You fucking proles! Corrupted
(He said) by goddamn money,
Let the devil take you, workers!

You are threadbare intellectuals,
November-Intellectuals, lousy intellectuals,
I remain the only prole,
I'll erect a monument to myself in revolutionary bronze,
I don't give a peep about your fat cat Fonz,
You are no longer competent."

So the emasculated intellectual cried,
The unmasked individual, the runaway intellectual,
And he swore bloody revenge on the people.
The true proles gave a hearty laugh
And said "You can decorate the cities
You destroyed as a politician!"

ALLER NÄCHTE SPIEGELBILD

Nun bin ich, Liebste, magisch deinem Leib verflochten.
Abendlauf der drängenden Gesichte spannt mich in dich ein
Und aller Nächte Spiegelbild ist Blühen deines Bluts.

Kaum leb ich noch im Spurengang von Zeichen, Geist und Sehnen
 nach dem blauen Stern:
So nah ruhn deine runden Glieder,
So tränkt mich Quelle deiner Zärtlichkeit.

Und wach und wie zu Ruhn geneigt
Kreist rotes Begehren.

Du Garten der Lust,
Entfessele Ring sinnlosen Seins!

Du Lerche, du Wald,
Blume und Strom, du trunken der Dinge:
Singe, wachse, blühe und fließe mir zu!

[WENN ICH WEISSE SCHMALE HÄNDE SEHE]

Wenn ich weisse schmale Hände sehe,
schlanke feine Finger,
deren Nägel rosig glänzen ...
denke ich an meiner Mutter Hände.
Hände,
die tausend Fältchen
eingekrallter Leiden,
sorgerfüllter Mühen
hart durchfurchen.
Wenn ich weisse schmale Hände sehe,
schlanke feine Finger,
deren Nägel rosig glänzen ...
denke ich an meiner Mutter Hände.

EVERY NIGHT A MIRROR

Now, my love, I am magically woven with your body.
The evening stream of faces further binds me to you
And the mirror image of every nightis the blooming of your blood.

I hardly live in the footsteps of signs, spirit, and longing
for the blue star anymore,
You slender limbs rest so near,
I am drenched in the fountain of your tenderness.

And red desire spins around me,
Awake and drifting off to sleep.

You garden of lust, release us
From the ring of meaningless being!

You larke, you forest,
Flower and stream, du drunk on objects
Sing, grow, blossom and flow toward me!

[WHEN I SEE WHITE SLENDER HANDS]

When I see white slender hands,
delicate slim fingers,
whose nails twinkle rosily ...
I think of my mother's hands,
Hands
roughly furrowed
with a thousand wrinkles
scarred with toil.
When I see white slender hands,
delicate slim fingers,
whose nails twinkle rosily ...
I think of my mother's hands.

AM FLUSS

Schneller wirbeln grüne Kreise,
Graue Flut spritzt weissen Gischt.
Möven tummeln sich zur Reise,
Stiebend Sägwerk keifend zischt.

Mittagswind bläht weite Röcke
Morscher Kahn stirbt blind im Sand.
Netze fächeln matt um Pflöcke.
Totes stösst der Strom zum Strand.

Der Kanal zerrinnt ins Weite.
Nebel schwimmt kulissenhaft.
Brücken rollen protzend Kraft.

Fluten stemmen sich an Klippen.
Glucksen Schaum aus Plätscherlippen.
Eine Welle sehnt Geleite.

WENN DU KOMMEN SOLLST

Komm' in des Frühlings duft'gem Blühen
Im goldnen Sonnenstrahlenglanz
Wenn in den Wäldern Funken sprühen
Und Elfen jauchzen wild im Tanz.

Komm' wenn des Sommers Atemgluten
Der Rosen junge Pracht verzehrt,
Die in der Liebesnacht verbluten
Da Mutterahnen sie geehrt.

Komm' in des Herbstes bangen Tagen,
Wenn uns umraschelt dürres Laub
Und unsere Herzen stumm verzagen
Der höhnenden Verwesung Raub.

Doch wenn des Winters weiche Flocken
Mich hüllen ein in Todesschlaf
Und in den Winkeln Qualen hocken
Die mein verglaster Blick noch traf ....

Dann sollst Du nicht mehr zu mir kommen
In meine tiefe Einsamkeit
Du darfst das Lachen nicht verlernen,
Geduld, der Frühling ist nicht weit

BY THE RIVER

Green circles whirling faster,
The gray tide spraying white froth.
Seagulls gather for their journey,
Sawmills spray their spitting hisses.

Midday wind billows distant skirts,
A rotting barge dies blind in the sand.
The nets fan out flat around the pier.
The current thrusts dead things to the shore.

The canal melts into the distance.
Fog swims on the stage.
Bridges roll, showing off their strength.

The tide struggles against the bluffs.
Gurgling froam from purling lips.
A wave only wants company.

WHEN YOU SHOULD ARRIVE

Come in the fragrant blossom of spring
In the golden glint of sunbeams
When sparks fly in the woods
And elfs dancing wildly with joy.

Come when the summer's ember breath
Consumes the young glory of roses,
Which bleed out on the night of love
Where our ancestral mothers had honored them.

Come on autumn's anxious days
When dry leaves crackle around us
And our hearts sink silent
In the presence of such scornful decay.

But when winter's gentle flakes
Fold me into their deathsleep
And in the corners of the room my eyes
Glaze and see agony itself on its haunches ....

Then you should no longer visit me
In my deepest solitude.
You must not unlearn your laughter,
Have patience, spring is not far.

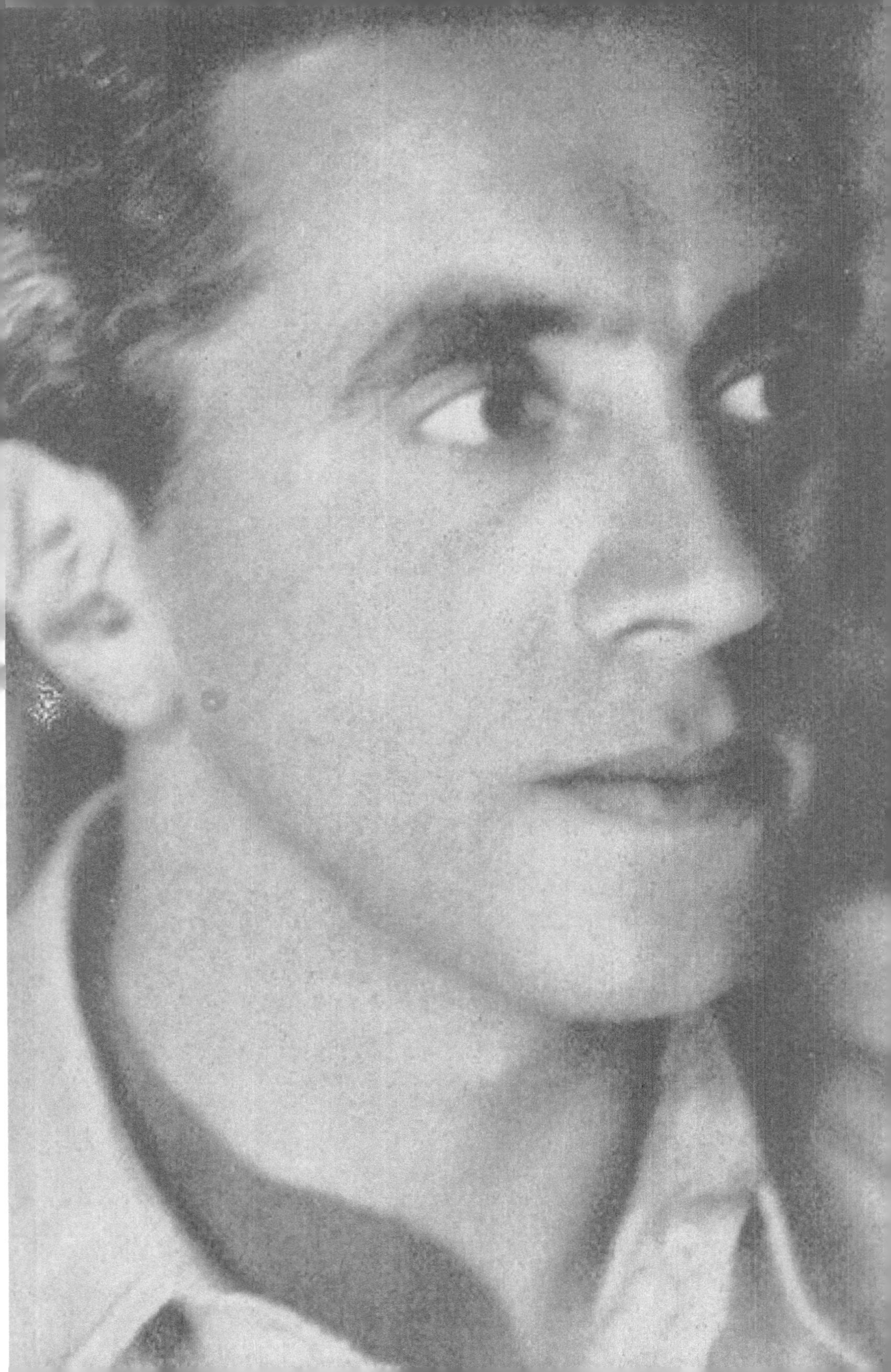

NOTES

Translator's notes are marked with a (tr.)

Notes adapted from James Jordan's *Previously Unpublished Poems of German Playwright Ernst Toller (1893 - 1939)* are marked with a (jj.)

Editorial notes from the Ernst Toller Society's edition of *Ernst Toller Sämtliche Werke Band 5* are marked with an (ed.)

The editors of the Ernst Toller Society's collected poetry are Dieter Distl, Martin Gerstenbräun, Torsten Hoffmann, James Jordan, Stephen Lamb, Peter Langemeyer, Karl Leydecker, Stefan Neuhaus, Michael Pilz, Kirsten Reimers, Christiane Schönfeld, Gerhard Scholz, Rolf Selbmann, Thorsten Unger und Irene Zanol. I am grateful for the editorial and archival work of all those mentioned above, and am particularly thankful for James Jordan's translation's of Ernst's uncollected poems and his brilliant archival work, and for Irene Zanol's incredible transatlantic support and love. I can't thank you enough for the copy of *Vormorgen*, which I treasure, and for your endless support in this endeavor. Thank you for making this possible.

GEDICHTE DER GEFANGENEN // POEMS OF THE IMPRISONED

(tr.) Originally published by the Kurt Wolff Verlag, München, 1921. It was the 84th edition in Der Jüngste Tag / The Youngest Day series. The subtitle *Ein Sonettenkreis* can be rendered a few ways: the slant-homophonic *Sonnenkreis* (sun-circle, or the stellar corona during an eclipse) lends us this "circle" or "crown," which, when combined with the *Sonetten* of *Sonettenkreis*, delivers either a crown of sonnets or a circle of sonnets, with the echo of a sonnet which stretches around the sun in solar eclipse.

(ed.) Toller's estate escaped destruction when his manuscripts were confiscated by the Nazi Party (NSDAP) in 1933 and were handed over to the NSDAP Central Archive (Now the Bundesarchiv Berlin). A folder written in Toller's hand which contained "Poems of the Imprisoned" had survived, along with other manuscripts and letters.

A letter from Ernst Toller to Kurt Wolff: March 20, 1921

Dear Herr Kurt Wolff,

my Easterly greeting is a strange request: Please read over the manuscript "Vormorgen." I would be very grateful if you would let me know soon whether you would like to print the booklet. [...] The manuscript was initially "twice as strong," but self-criticism forced me to "narrow it down". I have since quit the task. There may be verses that have their value beyond what is banned in form, that are not works of art - and yet are so much more. -

In letter from Kurt Wolff's secretary Annemarie von Puttkamer, she suggested the title *Vormorgen der Gefangenen* (*Dawn of the Imprisoned*) or *Wir müssen um das Sakrament der Erde ringen* (*We Must Struggle for the Sacrament of the Earth*), the last line of *Poems of the Imprisoned*, in a letter on April 17, 1921.

(Nr. 44), which was appended in the epigraph/subtitle of *Gedichte der Gefangenen*, was Toller's prison number at Niederschönenfeld .

The epigraph from Kleist was not actually written by Kleist, but by a forger, Karl Gustav Herwig, who had a series of publications in *Der Weltbühne*, including a series of "translations" of Kleist's allegedly unknown French-language letters.

16-17. Schlaflose Nacht / Sleepless Night

(ed.) Schritte / footsteps was once rendered Tropfen / droplets, but was crossed out. O, jeder Schlag / Oh, each beat - was changed to Schritt / step
(tr.) Another way to go about the last line in the first stanza would be to take a page out of Rilke, ever-sharpening claws. Fluch gesetzter Grenzen / Fuck set boundaries - Fluch is a kind of hex or a curse, I chose to render this as Fuck for the orthographic homophony, and for the sentiment.

16-17. Durchsuchung und Fesselung / Search and Capture

(ed.) A manuscript contained the note "Ernst Toller has sent us a few poems from the Niederschönenfeld prison. Today we are publishing two sonnets that will soon be published under the above title in a volume by Kurt Wolff." Another manuscript references this publication, saying "The latest issue of the journal Die Glocke (The Bells) contains two sonnets from a poet who was involved in the Bavarian Soviet Republic, Ernst Toller, who was imprisoned in the Niederschönenfeld fortress. These two sonnets are a new indictments against the Bavarian penal system. One can only hope that when Toller finally publishes a whole volume of his poems, humanity will finally have moved in beyond the fortress gates of Niederschönenfeld.

18-19. Wälder / Woods

(tr.) In my translation I have chosen to render *Ihr Buchenwälder, Dome der Bedrückten* as *Your Buchenwalds, domes of the oppressed*. This was an anachronistic decision in memory of Ernst's mother and sister, who were sentenced to concentration camps when Ernst was forced into exile from Germany to England and later to New York. Toller had been an open advocate against the rise of the NSDAP in its early days, fearful that Hitler would undo the successes of the Weimarer Republik with the stroke of a pen. The popularity of his plays was considered dangerous by the regime and Goebbels declared Ernst Toller Nazi Germany's 'political enemy number one.' Many of his works were burned during the book burnings of 1933. He continued to try to warn the world about the dangers of Nazism, arguing that the civil war in Spain was Nazi Germany's rehearsal for an approaching European war. Upon receiving word of his mother and sister's fate, Ernst shortly killed himself in a New York hotel, 1939.

18-19. Spaziergang der Sträflinge / Walk of the Convicts

(ed.) Dedicated to his fallen comrade Alois Wolmuth, who was executed by the Freikorps in Munich. (tr.) The paragraph is a significant unit of oppression in Toller's work. *Walk of the Convicts* shows the proletarian triumph over the tyranny of the paragraph despite their executed comrade. This image returns again in *Das Schwalbenbuch / The Book of Swallows*, see pages 50-51, 60-61. Paragraphs and screams. The paragraph is an illogical unit of frenetic bureaucracy, one that is incompatible to the enjambed mind of prisoners. A paragraph wants to reduce you to information, to identify you with the number on your cell (Nr. 44), to strip you down to phrenological measurements and surveilled movement.

22-23. Fabrikschornsteine am Vormorgen / Smokestacks at Dawn

(ed.) In addition to his handwritten manuscript, the poem has survived in a total of six different typed copies in Toller's estate, the material of which was confiscated by the Nazi Party in 1933 and escaped destruction in the main archive of the NSDAP (now in the Bundesarchiv in Berlin). One manuscript had been filed by Toller in a folder that was labeled "Early Poems" in his hand, and others were preserved in a folder entitled "Poems from Prison." But an extensive bundle of Toller's manuscripts have been preserved by Carl Hauptmann's estate. One is typed together with the poem *A Night in Prison* (a variant of the title *To Linger at Midnight*) on a sheet of paper with the additional heading: "Ernst Toller / Poems / written in the military prison 1918."

24-25. Die Mauer der Erschossenen / The Wall of the Executed

(ed.) This manuscript was contained in a folder of poems handwritten by Ernst Toller labeled "Poems from Prison." It is of note that the subtitle of this manuscript does not take the suppression of the Munich Soviet Republic of 1919 as a reference point for the events dealt with in the text - as it does in the typewritten print version - but rather the end of the Paris Commune of 1871, and thus, from an autobiographical reading, distracts in favor of the reference to a historical key event in the tradition and formation of left soviets (workers' councils). The subtitle *Stadelheim 1919* was previously *Paris 1871*, the year the Commune de Paris was founded and later seized. Both the Paris Commune and the Bavarian Soviet Republic lived short but impactful lives. (tr.) As Blanqui said "you confiscated the guns but our bullets have taken off," the trajectory of those bullets, what those bullets aimed at, was the sinister logic of capital itself. Even without their guns, those bullets are always flying toward that logic. We live forever in this recoil.

DAS SCHWALBENBUCH // THE BOOK OF SWALLOWS

42-43: Ein Freund starb in der Nacht.] A friend died in the Night.

(ed.) Biographically, this passage can be read as an allusion to the death of August Hagemeister, a fellow prisoner of Toller's, to whom the last chapter of Toller's *Justiz-Erlebnisse* is also dedicated.

50-51: Hölderlins Frühling / Hölderlin's Spring

(ed.) In many of Toller's writings and letters from prison he repeatedly refers to Friedrich Hölderlin and specifically quotes from his famous poem *Hälfte des Lebens*. (tr.) This is Kathleen Jamie's translation into Scots:

Hälfte des Lebens

Mit gelben Birnen hänget
Und voll mit wilden Rosen
Das Land in den See,
Ihr holden Schwäne,
Und trunken von Küssen
Tunkt ihr das Haupt
Ins heilignüchterne Wasser.

Weh mir, wo nehm' ich, wenn
Es Winter ist, die Blumen, und wo
Den Sonnenschein,
Und Schatten der Erde?
Die Mauern stehn
Sprachlos und kalt, im Winde
Klirren die Fahnen.

Midlife

Yellow with pears
Heavy with wild roses
The land hangs in the lake
Magnificent swans
Drunk with kisses
You dip your heads
In the holy sober water

Where will I find
Flowers this winter
And where will I find
The sunshine and shade
of the earth? Speechless and cold
The walls stand, and the weathercocks
Rattle in the wind

116-117: Epilogue

(ed.) The following footnote is taken from the chapter Nestersturm from *Justiz-Erlebnisse*, as an epilogue:

Swallows lived in a prisoner's cell for one summer. It was a pleasure for him. He tried to stammer about what they gave him. The prison administration didn't like what he wrote. Who can fathom the strict requirements of the prison administration! Enough, they didn't like it. They ordered the prisoner to leave his cell, with its barred window facing the east, and directed him carefllly and with paternal care to another, which received its poor light from the north and could not be a home to any swallow. In the next spring, in April, the swallows came again. Came from somewhere, from the jungle landscape and the dream of the sun, into the square of the bare, northern cell. They found a new inmate and were ready to provide the same comfort they gave their previous comrade. One day a book came into the first cell, thrown over the wall, out of reach of the guards. A few hours later, guards rumbled into the cell, tore down the almost completed nest with an indifferent, raw authority. How frightened the swallows were when they could no longer see their little apartment! With their beaks they traced the semicircle of the bottom of the nest, fluttered about in fear, peered into every corner of the cell, found nothing. They started building again on the next day. And again the guards destroyed the nest. The prisoner, a bricklayer from a Bavarian village, wrote this letter on May 18, 1924:

Lord Warden!

I asked the head overseer to leave this gentle and hard-won nest of these patient and extremely industrious little animals. I declare: they do not bother me in the least and do not harm me. I would like to hear from you. There are swallow nests in various prisons and they need not be destroyed with such severe punishment.

Sincerely, Ruppert Enzinger from Kolbermoor.

On May 21st, a board member of the prison, Hoffmann, gave the laconic notice: Swallows should build in the stable. There is enough space there. The nest, whose walls had since been rounded, fell under violation of this decree. The prisoner was shown one cell to the north, and the other was locked. Confused, passionately excited, the swallows began to build in three cells at the same time. Half of the nests were layered, but the wardens discovered them, and cruelty followed. The pair of swallows built in six cells. Who can know what they were doing! Maybe hope is there. Men gave them a nest out of compassion and a little kindness. The six nests were swept away. I don't know how many times construction and destruction followed one another. The battle had already lasted seven weeks; a heroic, glorious battle by the Bavarian legal advisor against the spirit of animal rebellion. The swallows stopped building for a few days, they had given up. This was spoken softly from prisoner to prisoner: You have found a place in the washroom between the drainpipes where no one can see it, not the eye of the guard who is scanning the bars from without, not the eyes of the overseers, who will pry into what is forbidden. Seldom was there such pure joy in the cell corridor. The swallows remained victorious in the battle against human malice. Every prisoner felt victorious. But the wardens, listening... One morning the washroom stared back, lifeless and empty. The swallows no longer built there. In the evening they flew into a cell, slept there, huddled close on the wire; flew away in the morning. Soon the male swallow came alone. The female swallow had died, probably because people had stopped her from retrieving her eggs, heavy with fruit.

VORMORGEN // TOWARD MORNING

122-123: Der Ringende / End of the Struggle

(ed.) A letter from Toller to Annemarie von Puttkamer, dated April 17, 1921, shows that he had originally planned to published *Der Ringende* in *Gedichte der Gefangenen*, but had decided to cut it.

122-123: Marschlied / Marching Song

(ed.) The title is handwritten in pencil; the typescript, which also has some minor corrections by Toller's hand, is preserved in a folder, the same folder from Toller with the inscription *Early Poems*. Another manuscript can be found in a bundle of poems that Toller probably sent to Carl Hauptmann in a letter. Between the title and the beginning of the text of one manuscript, the following introduction by the editor Franz Pfemfert is inserted:

If only I could finally hammer it into every naive reader that it wasn't about literature, the youngest or the oldest poetry! Here I am printing someone who, like Rudolf Leonhard, Hanns Heinz Ewers, doesn't have the technique to chant modernity; contemporary couplets out of time. No "poet" speaks here, no hopeful person from the Reinhard clique or the Wolfenstein ethic: a person speaks whose words stand behind his fate.

/ F. P.

130-131: An die Dichter / To the Poets

(ed.) This poem had been received as a supplement to a (possibly unsent) letter by Toller from the Munich military prison to Franz Pfemfert in the spring of 1918, in which he asked for this and other poems to be printed in the journal *Die Aktion*. The following editorial note has been added:

"Ernst Toller writes to us from the penal institution in Stadelheim. In unconditional and loyal comradeship we stand with him as someone who did not stop at the manifestation of the revolution on printed paper. The verses that he sends us and that we bring here to help him justify his cause, were written as early as 1918 in the military prison. But - he writes - they have the same meaning today. Today, when some writers became bloody revolutionary romantics and attacked those who earlier fought with them against the rape of humanity in the war and to whom the idea of humanity means more than an oppositional slogan."

130-1131: Den Müttern / The Mothers

(ed.) In April 1921, Toller wrote the Kurt Wolff Verlag suggesting to remove this poem from *Gedichte der Gefangenen*.

134-135: Deutschland / Germany

(ed.) This poem was also slated to be published in *Gedichte der Gefangenen* before Toller wrote to Annemarie von Puttkamer asking for it to be removed. The original title of the poem was *Durch das Gitter meiner Zelle... / Through the bars of my cell...*, which has remained its first line.

144-145: Lieder der Gefangenen / Songs of the Imprisoned

(tr.) Many of these poems are revisions from Toller's earlier drafts in Gedichte der Gefangenen, the most notable titular adaptation is that what were once poems are now songs. Many of these poems have been shortened, adjectives removed, and where some were once sonnets have since been snapped in two.

UN/VERÖFFENTLICHTE GEDICHTE // UN/PUBLISHED POEMS

(tr.) This last section consists of Ernst's Veröffentlichte Einzelgedichte and his Unveröffentlichte Einzelgedichte. I placed his published work before his unpublished work to give a sense of what has been left out. Many of the poems in this section have been workshopped alongside James Jordan's *Previously Unpublished Poems of German Playwright Ernst Toller (1893-1939)*. This book served has my lodestone, Jordan was a bright compass for me in this vastly overwhelming territory. I am extremely thankful for the work he has done collecting these works of Toller and for his brilliant prose translations, which my translations would be nothing without. Notes adapted from Jordan's commentary are labeled (jj.)

190-191: Steht eine Wacht in Frankreich / There stands a watch in France

(jj.) *Steht eine Wacht in Frankreich* comes from the earliest phase of Toller's participation in the war. In his autobiography he describes in detail the atmosphere of patriotic fervour amongst German nationals returning to their home soil upon the outbreak of hostilities in August 1914. As the exiles arrive in Switzerland, they burst out into a spontaneous renditions of *Deutschland über alles*, embracing each other in joy. This passage emphasises the absence of any critique as the euphoric conscripts-to-be, assured now of the Kaiser's impartiality, formulated in his famous dictum "Ich kenne keine Parteien mehr," (I no longer recognize any parties), intoxicate themselves with the phrases of unconditional patriotism. The Volk referred to in these poems is the German racial community to which Toller, at this stage in his development, desperately wanted to belong. Although German-ness provides the common identity, the actual process of unity is achieved only through the emergence of a potentially threatening external enemy. The love we find here is therefore not *Nächstensliebe* (Neighborly love), but rather the need for self-preservation within the collective. (Jordan, 45-46)

192-193: Frühling 1915 / Spring 1915

(jj.) The R.D. of the dedication is in all likelihood Richard Dehmel, who, though into his fifties, enlisted immediately for frontline duty in the war and wrote a considerable number of poems in praise of the German war effort. Just as Toller had in due course become perturbed by the war, Dehmel underwent similar doubts. Though Dehmel lapsed into eventual dissillusionment and bewilderment, Toller proceeded actively to oppose the war through his participation in the organization of the Munich munitions workers' strikes. His own physical and moral revulsion was to find effective expression in the collection *Verse vom Friedhof / Graveyard Verse* in *Vormorgen*. (Jordan, 48-49)

196-197: Sylvester 1916

(jj.) In March 1915, Toller volunteered for frontline duty and remained there until May 1916 when, digging in the trenches near Verdun, he found an unidentifiable corpse. This was the culmination of a series of traumatic experiences, and provoked a physical and mental collapse. He spent until September in hospitals and sanatoria, and in an invalid company at Mainz. He then signed up for the winter semester at Munich University, but it was not until January 4, 1917 that he was officially pronounced "kriegsuntauglich, aber dauernd arbeitsverwendungsfähig" (unfit for war, but still capable of work). Until New Year 1916/17, Toller had to live constantly with the possibility that he could be returned at any time to the front. The fear at that prospect is communicated vividly in this poem. (Jordan, 57)

198-199: Der Meister / The Master

(tr.) James Jordan's note on his translation regards many of the etymological neologistic problems in translating this poem. Any reader somewhat familiar with the styles of Else Lasker-Schüler or Paul Celan and their propensity for rending the language into compound adjectives will recognize this style. Jordan's note reads as follows:

"this poem poses a number of translation problems. Toller goes further than Lasker-Schüler in creating a series of neologisms which combine two words in new and striking collocation: *röckebesetzt* sets the scene in a lecture hall filled with female students; *schmuckzieren* combines *Schmuck*, jewelry, with *zieren*, to adorn; *centralfeurig* suggests fire emanating from the very insides of the lecturer; and *kunstverhalten* combines artifice with attitude or behavior. In addition there is *getagbucht* or equipped with a diary, that is to say, full of his own importance, and purpurt, which converts the adjective for crimson into a verb. *Brennesselrock* refers to the use of nettles during the war to make clothes in the absence of other materials." (Jordan, 73)

206-207: Ich weiss um Deine Tränen, Bruder / Brother Uprooted

(tr.) James Jordan appended the title *Der Entwurzelte / The Rootless One* to the poem in his collection; I have followed this scheme and called my translation *Brother Uprooted*.

(jj.) In *Der Fall Toller*, Frühwald and Spalek refer to a poetry reading given on January 25, 1918, where, among other texts, Toller read a poem called *Der Entwurzelte*. The emphasis on *Wurzeln* (roots) in the poem makes it likely that this is *Der Entwurzelte*. The poem, from the estate of the sculptor of Fritz Claus, deals with the search of its subject for healthy roots, here to be understood as social roots. (Jordan, 28)

208-209: Der Ruf / The Call

(jj.) While he lived in Munich from 1916 to 1917 and again from 1918 to 1919 Toller made friends with the minor Expressionist sculptor Fritz Claus. Little more is known of their relationship than that Toller dedicated *Nacht im Pristerwald* to Claus and gave him a number of other poems, some of which are now at the Deutsches Literaturarchiv Marbach. A note from Claus retained with the poems states that there were many others, but that they were so bad he burned them. (Jordan, 98)

210-211: Legende / Legend

(jj.) In January and February 1918 Toller was involved in raising support for strikes by munitions workers in Munich, as he tells in Eine Jugend in Deutschland:

(tr.) "I go to the strike meetings becuase I want to help, to do something; I distribute my poems because I believe that these verses, born of the horrors of war, strike them and accuse acuse them, distributing war poems among the women, the hospital and cripple scenes from my drama Die Wandlung."

(jj.) This poem could well have been one of those he distributed, as the second strophe refers directly to munitions factories, it is addressed to women and its aim is to discourage the production of arms. In order to achieve this, Toller writes a version of the myth current in both Germany and England at the time that women involved directly in war betray themselves in their role as the givers of life and are therefore cursed. The aim of the poem was to unsettle what Toller considered to be impressionable and susceptible women and to pressure them into a strike. Toller was well aware that the majority of the female munitions workers would be Bavarian Catholics. As a result, this poem is targeted not just at Christians but, with the prominent role played by the Virgin Mary, specifically at Catholics. Toller must have assumed that the working-class Catholics he was trying to influence maintained their beliefs on an instinctual rather than a critical level, because the poem is unashamedly superstitious in tenor. It is written too in a very simple and narrative manner, and Toller is clearly here trimming the Expressionist tenor of his other poetry in an attempt against alienating a working-class audience. (Jordan, 95)

218-219: Den in Dachau »standrechtlich« erschossenen Rotgardisten / To the Red Guards Executed "By Decree of the State" in Dachau

(jj.) In 1918 Toller made the acquaintance of Kurt Eisner and became involved in the politics of the USPD (Independent Social Democratic Party of Germany) after the declaration by Eisner of a Bavarian Republic in November of that year. After disastrous election results in 1919, Eisner was murdered on the way to hand in his resignation in February. There followed to months of political ferment in Munich resulting in the proclamation in early April 1919 of a Councils Republic led by Toller. This first Councils Republic was ousted barely a week later by a second council under the communist Eugen Leviné. This provoked the national government into sending a force of Reichswehr and Freikorps troops to suppress the revolution in the Bavarian Capital.

The savagery of this operation, in which over one thousand people lost their lives, is meticulously and chillingly detailed by Emil Julius Gumbel, at that stage a professor at Heidelberg University and later to establish many of the principles of statistical analysis. Using Gumbel's approach as his model, Toller published after his release from prison the volume *Justiz-Erlebnisse*, which described in detail many of the crimes committed in the retaking of Munich and exposed the harshness of the military regime. This poem refers to an incident of which we have no clear record, but which must have occured during the battle at Dachau, one of the most bitter engagements between government and revolutionary troops, and in which Toller led the forces of the Councils Republic.

Although summary execution — with later claims of courts martial having been held — was a normal practice for the late Weimar forces, Toller sought during his brief command to set an example of leniency and understanding towards the captured White troops. He defied orders from his Commander-in-Chief, Egelhofer, to execute 41 captured government troops at Dachau on April 16, allowing them instead free passage in the hope of changing their minds towards the revolution:

(tr.) "No matter how brutal the laws of civil war may be, I know the counter-revolution in Berlin executed their red prisoners without mercy. We fight for a fairer world. We demand humanity. We have to be human." (GW IV, 147) Wryly, Toller then relates that the soldiers immediately rejoined the government forces. (Jordan, 103-104)

220-221: Gefängnis und Zeit / Prison and Time

(tr.) There is a manuscript discrepancy between James Jordan's *Poems* and the version preserved in the *Sämtliche Werke*. I have chosen to translate the poem as it is preserved in the collected works, but James Jordan has reconstructed the poem from removed lines, which I will reproduce here:

Was ist ein Jahr und was ist eine Stunde
Im Acker Zeit, der brach zu unsern Füßen liegt
Der wie ein immergleich Klageton sich wiegt,
Gesetz und Form gestaltenlos entwunden.

Einst war die Zeit wie eine seltsame Legende
Die in brokatnem Gewand das Wunder hüllte

Wir wußten, daß es köstlich uns erfüllte,
Wenn unsere Hand den goldenen Schlüssel fände

Nun tönt der Glockenschlag der Uhren toten Klang
Wir sind vertrieben aus dem Kreis der Zeit
Wir sind gestoßen in die antlitzlose Finsterheit.

Wie Nebelfetzen flattern wir im Käfiggang,
Von Wächteraugen spähenden bedrängt.
O köstlich wird die Welt, die reich uns einst beschenkt.–

(Jordan, 125). This reconstructed poem I have translated thus:

What is a year and what is an hour,
in the time of the field that lies fallow under our feet,
Which rocks like an evergreen complaint,
Gestalt unwound from law and form.

Time was once an curious tale
That kept its miracle folded under brocade garments.
We knew it would satisfy us, deliciously
If our hand could find the golden key.

Now the clocks strike death,
We are cast from the sphere of time
Thrust into the faceless dark.

Like shredded fog we flit through our caged corridors,
Weighed down by the heavy eyes of the warden.
But O, the delicious world that once filled us with its plenty.

222-223: Für Erich Mühsam / For Erich Mühsam

(jj.) During there political work in Munich both before and during the Councils Republic, Toller and Mühsam had come into conflict. Politically they had come from very different directions: Toller was a pacifist turned socialist under the influence of Gustav Landauer's belief in peaceful spiritual transformation as the basis of social change; the anarchist Mühsam, constantly searhing for the ideological nexus between communism and anarchism, was deeply sympathetic to the plight of the proletariat and prepared to justify radical action in the cause of political justice. Tempermentally, too, they seemed irreconcilable: Mühsam was sensitive but tended to be brutally candid in his opinions and was prone to withering sarcasm; Toller was highly vulnerable to criticism and sought compromise before conflict and regarded himself seriously.

These tensions grew when Mühsam joined Toller in prison in Niederschönenfeld in October 1920. In his diaries Mühsam notes immediately the formation of a clique of 'intellectuals' around Toller, whom Mühsam criticizes for his vanity and need for publicity, but whose purity of thought and principle he admires. Matters came to a head when several inmates paid by the prison authorities for cleaning the cells were expected to clean additional cells for no extra reward. Mühsam and his supporters called a strike and soon the rubbish began to pile up in the corridors. When Toller and his associates cleared away some of the rubbish, Mühsam accused them of strike-breaking, a charge against wish they vigorously defended themselves on the grounds that no official strike had been called...

Toller makes reference to Kain. *Zeitschrift für Menschlichkeit,* the political and cultural journal started by Mühsam in 1911 as a platform for his own views, which were often so radical and polemical that they failed to get published. The reference to November-Intellektuelle is an adaptation of the term *Novemberverbrecher,* used by the extreme right to describe the socialist politicians (and, by extension, communists, Jews, etc) who made peace in 1918 when, in the right's view, Germany was on the brink of victory...

Mühsam was deeply moved by Toller's release in 1924: "Wir sind als sehr gute intime Freunde geschieden und werden es bleiben" (We have departed as very good intimate friends, and so we will remain). Toller's recollections of revolution and prison were published from exile in *Eine Jugend in Deutschland* (1933) and the *Briefe aus dem Gefängnis* (1935). There is no trace in either volume of the bitterness between them in the early stages of their imprisonment. Mühsam's courage in the face of brutal treatment by the SS in the Oranienburg concentration camp was to find a lasting memorial in Toller's final play, *Pastor Hall,* completed only one year before the latter's suicide. (Jordan, 129-132)

INDEX OF TITLES AND FIRST LINES IN ENGLISH

* poems labled with an asterisk indicate revised versions of poems that previously appeared in *Poems of the Imprisoned*, Ernst edited these, often shorting them, and published their revisions in *Vormorgen*.

INDEX OF TITLES AND FIRST LINES IN GERMAN

ABOUT THE AUTHOR

ERNST TOLLER (1893-1939) was a Jewish anarchist working in Munich, and briefly served as the president of the Bavarian Soviet Republic (Münchner Räterepublik / Munich Workers' Republic), which was predominantly organized by poets and playwrights, also known as "the regime of coffeehouse anarchists." When the monarchy collapsed in November, Toller helped to organize the Bavarian Soviet in Munich and led street troops against the Freikorps and shock troops sent to the suppress the uprising. He was arrested for high treason and sentenced to five years in prison, which he first spent in the correctional facility in Munich (Stadelheim) before he was transferred to Niederschönenfeld in 1920. While in prison, he authored multiple plays and wrote two volumes of poetry, Gedichte der Gefangenen / Poems of the Imprisoned (1921) and Das Schwalbenbuch / The Book of Swallows (1924). After his release he was forced into exile from Germany due to mounting tensions of the Nazi regime. Upon receiving word that his mother and sister had been sent to concentration camps, he committed suicide in his room at the Mayflower Hotel in New York on May 22, 1939.

ABOUT THE TRANSLATOR

MATHILDA CULLEN is a poet and translator. She is a central committee member of Woe Eroa, a press dedicated to printing and developing an explicitly Marxist, militant poetics. Her works include *Vormorgen: The Collected Poems of Ernst Toller* (The Operating System, 2021) and *Stanzas for Four Hands: An Ophanim* with Dominick Knowles (woe eroa, 2021), *The Horizon is a Kettle: Notes on the Negative Lyric*. Find more of her at mathildacullen.com or being annoying on social media.

OF PROLES & PARAGRAPHS
AN OS [RE:CON]VERSATION WITH MATHILDA CULLEN, POET & TRANSLATOR

Greetings comrade! Thank you for talking to us about your process today! Can you introduce yourself, in a way that you would choose?

I'm Mathilda Cullen.

Why do you work in translation?

Because I like to be wrong. Because I'm wrong most of the time. Because after a while it's not about that at all.

In addition or instead of "translator," what other titles or affiliations do you prefer/ feel are more accurate? What other work are you doing in the world these days?

Poet is the only appellation suitable for this compulsive delirium. *Translator* suggests I've succeeded at something, have converted a product from one form to another, have ferried it across a river and have had it approved by customs, am presenting you with a neatly wrapped package. Translation isn't a good word for this bizarre endeavor because it's etymology has always been steeped in transference and conquest.

What do you see as your cultural and social role (in the literary / artistic / creative community and beyond)? How does this interface with what you do as a translator and/or in your pedagogy?

In the hopes that one day I will work to work. That there is meaning in cultural labor beyond the market, beyond profit and rent. Much of this work took place during the COVID-19 pandemic, when, for a short while, many of my friends, myself included, received unemployment benefits that acted as a sort of proto- universal basic income. This freed us from the dangers of work (physically, mentally) for the time being, and, contrary to popular belief, we did not find ourselves without work. There was rest, of course, whatever can approximate rest right now, lots of naps. I had a sleeping schedule not dissimilar from right now. Melatonin puts me to sleep around 1am. I get a couple nice hours of sleep, wake around 4 or 5, will go downstairs, make some coffee, maybe watch an episode of *Battlestar Galactica* and dive into whatever research I was doing the night before. I get a few hours of work done thanks to whatever insomnia this is. Then around 9 or 10 I'll notice Margo shifting around (she tends to move every now again and will, like clockwork, kick the mock-nightstand next to her as she curls up). This will, undoubtedly, make me smile, and since Coffee #1 has likely worn off I'll probably decide to join her for a couple more hours. Then the day will pass in a similar fashion to this. More coffee, an occasional meal, more naps. This is a life outside of fruitless labor. I work, of course, but is it for myself? Am I a *self-starter*? There is a meme going around right now, "Damn shawty, beyond the baricade is there a world you long to see?" featuring two stickdrawn figures, one of them smiling before the flag of the Paris Commune. My parents have often posed the question of my work in terms of what is marketable. And sure, this book is likely in your hands because you bought it (or you're reading a PDF I sent you, or you downloaded it for free). I don't think the labor that is involved in poetry and artistic practices maps very well onto our received notions of labor as a means to an end (rent, food, etc). For that brief period of UBI, my friends and I had more money we had ever earned in our lives. We had a newfound comfort, one we didn't think the current infrastructure was capable of (and, has since proven itself incapable). This was a utopian accident, a calculation and PR nightmare. All of a sudden, anyone could have anything they asked for. *You can have anything you ask for, ask for everything.*

Talk about the process or instinct to move this project into book form. How and why did this happen? Have you had this intention for a while? What encouraged and/or confounded this (or a book, in general) coming together?

I originally published *Poems of the Imprisoned* as a short run edition printed in my dorm room at college. Ernst had been out of print for nearly a century and I had ink and paper. This was print. I spent my time at the library or at the coffeeshop on campus with papers sprawled around me. Tabs of dictionaries opened on my laptop; transcribing, crossing out, drawing lines. It was more a process of discovery than it was ever an intended transmission. Those first translations are sloppy, for sure, but they're beautiful in that they were my first attempts to make sense of Ernst, my first grappling with him. Historically, most of my efforts in language learning have been through music, through writing down the lyrics to a song and making a diagram in translation around them (this is perhaps a rudimentary form of the interlinear translation as suggested by Benjamin). I likely would not have continued with this project had it not been for the success of that chapbook I stapled together in my dorm and shipped to friends everywhere. I submitted that manuscript to the OS late 2019, and some months later got an email I was in all honesty not expecting. Elæ and I discussed the possibility of expanding *Poems of the Imprisoned* to include the whole of Ernst's published work, and all of a sudden I had a year of him ahead of me. I've been very grateful to Elæ for all their support and patience with me in this project, all the emails I've sent them in the middle of the night with news of some development. I'm also incredibly grateful to the generous support of Irene Zanol of the Ernst Toller Society, who provided me with a full edition of Ernst's poems including those unpublished and collected by James Jordan. The book happened because nobody said no. And as translators love to say, any and all errors herein are mine entirely.

What practices or structures (if any) do you use in the creation of your work, beyond this project? Have certain teachers or instructive environments, or readings/writings/work of other creative people informed the way you work/write?

I was lucky to have a cadre of German teachers through middle school and high school who encouraged me to stick with the language. I'm deeply grateful for the efforts of Frau Makris, Frau Siebel, Herr Sidwell, and Frau Cardi for instilling a love of German in my deeply depressed and repressive teenage self. German and dabbling in other languages throughout high school was likely a coping mechanism for one of the most difficult emotional periods of my life. I'm particularly grateful to Herr Sidwell, who, upon spotting my then-just-out cracked-egg of a self in the Starbucks in our town, sat with me to discuss the translation I was working on.

In terms of my practice it's rather fitting for someone of my generation. When I sit down to work I have five tabs open and three windows. The first is the base text, typically on the left and left undisturbed. The next is the working document, typically to my right, with enough space to fit the width of a line. And lastly is the research window, where I have as many tabs open as necessary, all weapons free. This window will likely have a few choice dictionaries at the ready, Wiktionary among them, and Google Translate. I'll typically read a line and toss it in there just to see what it spits back. Sometimes it's decent, other times it has no fucking clue what's going on grammatically and I've gotta step in. This step is a kind of linguistic grounding, a survey to see which parts of the line I really need to hone in on. The next few (few?) minutes are spent dictionary hopping trying to find words I don't know or words whose meanings may be manifold. This type of hopscotch translation has been helpful to me in creating a "workflow" that I can at most times dive back into. Even if it is draining, it's a practice I'd be doing anyway.

What does this book DO (as much as what it says or contains)?

This book is an artifact against forgetting; a forgotten history of a nearly forgotten poet. A poet whose works have only been translated by a few toward English in the past century. Of these translators, the only ones published in print were David Grunwald and James Jordan, there have been a handful of blogs that have selected bits of his work and translated them as well. There has yet to be a full book of Toller's verse in English, nor even a book in German to circulate his poetry in PDF form or a cheap paperback. I was lucky to find some good scans of the original prints, written in that old sharp and squiggly German print. I got real good at reading that while working on the *Schwalbenbuch*, even if it pissed me off, it was a genuine conversation. I feel good to have put myself into this effort for two years. To have it materialize into something whose future I won't know, don't even want to know. I hope people enjoy these poems. I hope someone else comes along and tears me to shreds.

What does it mean to make books in this time, and what are your thoughts around shifting into digital books/objects and digital access in general?

Big fan of digital books, most of the work I read and put out is digital, mainly because the infrastructure to print and distribute books is so fucked. I hope that changes, I have hopes it will change. In general I think the shift to digital media is good. Saves money, pecks at the extractive labor of warehouses, puts the onus of distributing elsewhere. It feels liberating to throw a PDF into the void. Who the fuck is gonna read it anyway.

Let's talk a little bit about the role of translation, creative practice and community in social and political activism, so present in our daily lives as we face the often sobering, sometimes dangerous realities of the Capitalocene. How does your process, practice, or work otherwise interface with or reflect these conditions?

I think my translation practice spans a few types of -isms. First, there is this kind, the Toller-kind, where I want to *translate* in the sense translation has always been used. Then there is someone like Emmy Hennings, whose own politics and misrepresentation and obscurity require an entirely different kind of translation. I think the de Campos brothers hit something on the head with *transcriação* or transcreation, (it reminds me of Paulo Freire's *conscientização*, probably because they both have that beautiful *ção* flaire to them). Anyway, when I translate Emmy it's not translation, it's transcreation (which sounds cringy as a trans person, I know), maybe zaum gets it, maybe the asemic painters know what I mean. I try to translate Emmy in as many ways as I can at once. I want the poem splayed open. Want, like Nabokov, footnotes upon footnotes, a second book full of footnotes. That part of my practice is very visual and is something I hope to expand and fill rooms with. But for right now it's digital and it's very generative. You'll hear more about that elsewhere.

I'd be curious to hear some of your thoughts on the challenges we face in speaking and publishing across lines of race, age, ability, class, privilege, social/cultural background, gender, sexuality (and other identifiers) within the community as well as creating and maintaining safe spaces, vs. the dangers of remaining and producing in isolated "silos" and/or disciplinary and/or institutional bounds?

I had a recurring waking auditory hallucination that I was being interviewed on some German podcast about why I, a trans woman, was fit to translate Ernst Toller. I had some convoluted answer that made sense in my hallucinated fog: *Ernst Toller's autobiography* Eine Jugend in Deutschland *is translated into English as* I was a German, *which is not the title, obviously, but gets to something me and Ernst share. For his whole life he longed to be a part of the German Volk, just like I longed to hide myself in cisness. There was an outbreak, the war came to his front door, he couldn't live with this desire to assimilate and neither could I. Like Ernst, I was something and have become something else. I can't compare my life to Ernst's, I have not experienced the trenches like him, did not lead a Soviet of Bavarians into war to defend Munich (yet), but we both experienced our own kind of Wandlung (transformation), and it's in this way that we are kin. Entwurzelten.*

Is there anything else we should have asked, or that you want to share?

I think I'm happy with what I've said. I will probably read over it and regret it and wish I said more, but in the spirit of the archive I will leave some erotic fervor and fluorish.

ABOUT GLOSSARIUM : UNSILENCED TEXTS

The Operating System's GLOSSARIUM: UNSILENCED TEXTS series was established in early 2016 in an effort to recover silenced voices outside and beyond the canon, seeking out and publishing contemporary translations, translingual projects, and little or un-known out of print texts, in particular those under siege by restrictive regimes and silencing practices in their home (or adoptive) countries. We are committed to producing dual-language versions whenever possible.

Few, even avid readers, are aware of the startling statistic reporting that less than three percent of all books published in the United States, per UNESCO, are works in translation. Less than one percent of these (closer to 0.7%) are works of poetry and fiction. You can imagine that even less of these are experiemental or radical works, in particular those from countries in conflict with the US or where funding is hard to come by.

Other countries are far, far ahead of us in reading and promoting international literature, a trend we should be both aware of and concerned about—how does it come to pass that attentions in the US become so myopic, and as a result, so under-informed? We see the publication of translations, especially in volume, to be a vital and necessary act for all publishers to require of themselves in the service of a more humane, globally aware, world. By publishing 7 titles in 2019, we raised the number of translated books of literature published in the US that year *by a full percent*. We plan to continue this growth as much as possible.

The dual-language and translingual titles either in active circulation or forthcoming in this series include Arabic-English, Farsi-English, Polish-English, French-English, Faroese-English, German-English, Danish-English, Martinican Creole-English, Yaqui Indigenous American translations, and Yiddish-English as well as a host of Spanish-English translations (from Cuba, Argentina, Mexico, Uruguay, Bolivia, and Puerto Rico).

The term 'Glossarium' derives from latin/greek and is defined as 'a collection of glosses or explanations of words, especially of words not in general use, as those of a dialect, locality or an art or science, or of particular words used by an old or a foreign author.' The series is curated by OS Founder and Creative Director Elæ with the help of global collaborators and friends.

ABOUT KIN(D)* TEXTS & PROJECTS

Vormorgen is a simultaneous publication under the OS & Liminal Lab's KIN(D)* imprint, a dedication to continuously publishing the work of trans and gender nonconforming creative practitioners.

The Operating System uses the language "print document" to differentiate from the book-object as part of our mission to distinguish the act of documentation-in-book-FORM from the act of publishing as a backwards-facing replication of the book's agentive *role* as it may have appeared the last several centuries of its history. Ultimately, I approach the book as TECHNOLOGY: one of a variety of printed documents (in this case, bound) that humans have invented and in turn used to archive and disseminate ideas, beliefs, stories, and other evidence of production.

Ownership and use of printing presses and access to (or restriction of printed materials) has long been a site of struggle, related in many ways to revolutionary activity and the fight for civil rights and free speech all over the world. While (in many countries) the contemporary quotidian landscape has indeed drastically shifted in its access to platforms for sharing information and in the widespread ability to "publish" digitally, even with extremely limited resources, the importance of publication on physical media has not diminished. In fact, this may be the most critical time in recent history for activist groups, artists, and others to insist upon learning, establishing, and encouraging personal and community documentation practices. Hear me out.

With The OS's print endeavors I wanted to open up a conversation about this: the ultimately radical, transgressive act of creating PRINT / DOCUMENTATION in the digital age. It's a question of the archive, and of history: who gets to tell the story, and what evidence of our life, our behaviors, our experiences are we leaving behind? We can know little to nothing about the future into which we're leaving an unprecedentedly digital document trail — but we can be assured that publications, government agencies, museums, schools, and other institutional powers that be will continue to leave BOTH a digital and print version of their production for the official record. Will we?

As a (rogue) anthropologist and long time academic, I can easily pull up many accounts about how lives, behaviors, experiences — how THE STORY of a time or place — was pieced together using the deep study of correspondence, notebooks, and other physical documents which are no longer the norm in many lives and practices. As we move our creative behaviors towards digital note taking, and even audio and video, what can we predict about future technology that is in any way assuring that our stories will be accurately told – or told at all? How will we leave these things for the record? In these documents we say:

WE WERE HERE, WE EXISTED, WE HAVE A DIFFERENT STORY

- Elæ Moss, Founder/Creative Director

RECENT & FORTHCOMING

OS PRINT::DOCUMENTS and PROJECTS, 2019-21

2020-21

Institution is a Verb: A Panoply Performance Lab Compilation - Esther Neff, Ayana Evans, Tsedaye Makonnen and Elizabeth Lamb, editors.
Vidhu Aggarwal - Daughter Isotope
Johnny Damm - Failure Biographies
Power ON - Ginger Ko
Spite - Danielle Pafunda
Acid Western - Robert Balun

KIN(D)* TEXTS AND PROJECTS

Intergalactic Travels: Poems from a Fugutive Alien - Alan Pelaez Lopez
HOAX - Joey De Jesus [Kin(d)*]
RoseSunWater - Angel Dominguez [Kin(d)*/Glossarium]
Bodies of Work - Elæ Moss & Georgia Elrod

GLOSSARIUM: UNSILENCED TEXTS AND TRANSLATIONS

Steven Alvarez - Manhatitlán [Glossarium]
Híkurí (Peyote) - José Vincente Anaya (tr. Joshua Pollock)
Ernst Toller's "Vormorgen" & Emmy Hennings - Radical Archival Translations - Mathilda Cullen [Glossarium x Kin(d)*; German-English]
Black and Blue Partition ('Mistry) - Monchoachi (tr. Patricia Hartland) [Glossarium; French & Antillean Creole/English]

IN CORPORE SANO

Hypermobilities - Ellen Samuels
Goodbye Wolf-Nik DeDominic

2019

Ark Hive-Marthe Reed
I Made for You a New Machine and All it Does is Hope - Richard Lucyshyn
Illusory Borders-Heidi Reszies
A Year of Misreading the Wildcats - Orchid Tierney
Of Color: Poets' Ways of Making | An Anthology of Essays on Transformative Poetics - Amanda Galvan Huynh & Luisa A. Igloria, Editors

KIN(D)* TEXTS AND PROJECTS

A Bony Framework for the Tangible Universe-D. Allen [In Corpore Sano]
Opera on TV-James Brunton
Hall of Waters-Berry Grass
Transitional Object-Adrian Silbernagel

GLOSSARIUM: UNSILENCED TEXTS AND TRANSLATIONS

Śnienie / Dreaming - Marta Zelwan/Krystyna Sakowicz, (Poland, trans. Victoria Miluch)
High Tide Of The Eyes - Bijan Elahi (Farsi-English/dual-language) trans. Rebecca Ruth Gould and Kayvan Tahmasebian
In the Drying Shed of Souls: Poetry from Cuba's Generation Zero Katherine Hedeen and Víctor Rodríguez Núñez, translators/editors
Street Gloss - Brent Armendinger with translations of Alejandro Méndez, Mercedes Roffé, Fabián Casas, Diana Bellessi & Néstor Perlongher (Argentina)
Operation on a Malignant Body - Sergio Loo (Mexico, trans. Will Stockton)[In Corpore Sano]
Are There Copper Pipes in Heaven - Katrin Ottarsdóttir (Faroe Islands, trans. Matthew Landrum)

DOCUMENT

/däkyəmənt/

First meant "instruction" or "evidence," whether written or not.

noun - a piece of written, printed, or electronic matter that provides information or evidence or that serves as an official record
verb - record (something) in written, photographic, or other form
synonyms - paper - deed - record - writing - act - instrument

[*Middle English, precept, from Old French, from Latin documentum, example, proof, from docre, to teach; see dek- in Indo-European roots.*]

Who is responsible for the manufacture of value?

Based on what supercilious ontology have we landed in a space where we vie against other creative people in vain pursuit of the fleeting credibilities of the scarcity economy, rather than freely collaborating and sharing openly with each other in ecstatic celebration of MAKING?

While we understand and acknowledge the economic pressures and fear-mongering that threatens to dominate and crush the creative impulse, we also believe that ***now more than ever we have the tools to redistribute agency via cooperative means,*** fueled by the fires of the Open Source Movement.

Looking out across the invisible vistas of that rhizomatic parallel country we can begin to see our community beyond constraints, in the place where intention meets resilient, proactive, collaborative organization.

Here is a document born of that belief, sown purely of imagination and will. When we document we assert. We print to make real, to reify our being there. When we do so with mindful intention to address our process, to open our work to others, to create beauty in words in space, to respect and acknowledge the strength of the page we now hold physical, a thing in our hand, we remind ourselves that, like Dorothy: *we had the power all along, my dears.*

the PRINT! DOCUMENT SERIES

is a project of

the trouble with bartleby

in collaboration with

the operating system

www.ingramcontent.com/pod-product-compliance
Lightning Source LLC
Chambersburg PA
CBHW030320100526
44592CB00010B/500
* 9 7 8 1 9 4 6 0 3 1 6 9 3 *